19th Century *Elegant* Lighting

4880 Lower Valley Road, Atglen, PA 19310 USA

19th Century *Elegant* Lighting

Argand, Sinumbra, and Solar Lamps

Gerald T. Gowitt

Library of Congress Control Number: 2001098863

Designed by Bonnie M. Hensley
Cover design by Bruce M. Waters
Type set in Lydian BT/Zapf Humanist BT

ISBN: 0-7643-1514-5
Printed in China
1 2 3 4

Published by Schiffer Publishing Ltd.
4880 Lower Valley Road
Atglen, PA 19310
Phone: (610) 593-1777; Fax: (610) 593-2002
E-mail: Schifferbk@aol.com
Please visit our web site catalog at **www.schifferbooks.com**
We are always looking for people to write books on new and related subjects. If you have an idea for a book, please contact us at the above address.

This book may be purchased from the publisher.
Include $3.95 for shipping.
Please try your bookstore first. You may write for a free catalog.

In Europe, Schiffer books are distributed by
Bushwood Books
6 Marksbury Avenue
Kew Gardens
Surrey TW9 4JF England
Phone: 44 (0) 20 8392 8585; Fax: 44 (0) 20 8392 9876
E-mail: Bushwd@aol.com
Free postage in the UK. Europe: air mail at cost.

Dedication

This book is dedicated to my son, Thomas, my daughter, Gail, and my wife, Vivian, who have brought much happiness to me over the years.

Acknowledgments

Grant and Mary Oakes, Service Guide Collection, Cortland, Ohio for their advice, patience, and allowing access to many of the lighting devices illustrated in this book. Without their cooperation this publication would not have been possible.

Vivian L. Gowitt, Lawrenceville, Georgia for doing the research, typing the manuscript, laying out the cover and putting up with her husband, the author, during this most trying time.

Also:

Heinz Baumann, Buffalo, New York
Robert Brooker, Native Soil, Boston, Massachusetts
R. Curt Chinnici, Philadelphia, Pennsylvania
Robyn Christensien, The Boston Historical Society and Museum, Boston, Massachusetts
Colleen Couture, Old Sturbridge Village Research Library, Sturbridge, Massachusetts
Larry DeCan, Seattle, Washington
Susan Garwood-Delong, Archives Department, Carleton College, Northfield, Minnesota
Michael Durrant, Picture Library, Victoria and Albert Museum, London, England
Victoria Emmanuel, Birmingham Museum and Art Gallery, Birmingham, England
Charity Galbreath, Peabody Essex Museum, Salem, Massachusetts
Iain Harrison, Picture Library, Birmingham Museum and Art Gallery, Birmingham, England
R. M. Harvey, Guildhall Library, Corporation of London, London, England
Tammy Hopkins, Lawrenceville, Georgia, for technical assistance with production of the manuscript
Doreen Hopwood, Genealogist, Birmingham Local History Studies, Birmingham, England
Garrison Kingsley, New Orleans, Louisiana
Ian Lekus, Special Collections Library, Duke University, Durham, North Carolina
Dan Pressly, Cortland, Ohio, for photographing the 1850 Hooper Catalogue
Peter Semus, Hove, England
Keith Sequeira, Focus Atlanta, Atlanta, Georgia
Prabha Shad, Science Museum Library, South Kensington, London, England
Spruance Library, Mercer Museum, Bucks County Historical Society, Doylestown, Pennsylvania
Guy Tennille, Focus Atlanta, Atlanta, Georgia
John Whybrow Ltd, Birmingham, England

Contents

Introduction

The impetus to write this book occurred on late Thursday afternoon, July 2, 1999 while driving from Cortland to Sandusky, Ohio in a terrible rainstorm. I had just witnessed the most wonderful display of Argand, sinumbra, and solar lighting devices imaginable. Many of these lamps were in original condition, nearly all had the proper burner, and very few were electrified. Room after room contained rare and unusual lighting, each piece having its own story and presented with endless enthusiasm by a master collector.

My wife and I had been collecting composite kerosene lamps for about two years and we had a working knowledge of that subject. However, I knew virtually nothing about colza, lard, and sperm whale oil burning devices. In an afternoon I had been given a whirlwind crash course in lighting manufacturers, metal castings, glass production, and the burning of heavy oils. I immediately fell in love with this charismatic and relatively under-explored segment of lighting.

While I was convinced a text on this subject was needed and feasible, others were not so enthralled. Over a year would pass before I could arrange a contract with the publisher and gain photographic access to the appropriate lighting collections. During this time I gathered whatever data was available concerning Argand, sinumbra, and solar lighting devices. This information was mostly found in scattered bits and pieces: a sentence or two in one book, a solitary picture in another text, etc. Clearly, one had to struggle to obtain meaningful information of any significant depth on the subject. For the author, this paucity of data was good as it fortified the necessity of the project. Nearly everyone wants to see more photographs and reference material. I hope this work will be used as a reference manual concerning certain aspects of these lighting devices for many years to come.

As will be seen, Argand, sinumbra, and solar lamps were introduced at different times during the first half of the nineteenth century, or what is referred to by some lighting authorities as the First Period (see below). Never in widespread use, today they are relatively scarce, especially in original condition. This book is intended to serve as a pictorial guide to these lighting devices and their manufacturers for beginner, mid level, and advanced collectors. Brief histories for some of the better known lighting manufacturers are given. The reader is presented a variety of different style lamps of the first half of the nineteenth century through the use of photographs, old etchings, and literature of the time. The text and pictorial descriptions emphasize the aesthetic and historical points of view.

The book is not meant to be an exhaustive technical dissertation concerning burner function, glass manufacturing, or metallurgy. In fact, a concise treatise on heavy oil burners is sorely needed and long overdue. The other subjects have been thoroughly addressed elsewhere and the reader is directed to those publications.

The author realizes that some of the lighting devices depicted in this text have undergone varying degrees of reconditioning. With some of these lamps nearing two hundred years of age, many required some restoration in order to maintain their historical importance, preservation, and appreciation. Where possible, mention is made of the extent of restoration. Unless otherwise specified, all lighting fixtures are shown with glass shades (globes) of the proper time period.

A Word About Lighting Trade Catalogues

As many may already know, pre-kerosene lighting trade cards and catalogues are exceedingly rare. The author has attempted to give the reader the benefit of the only known 1850 Henry N. Hooper and Company catalogue as well as selected excerpts from the 1856 Starr, Fellows and 1860 Dietz publications. In addition, illustrations of the Messenger Company patterns of the 1840s and from other lighting manufacturers of the 1820s are utilized. Invaluable information is contained within these documents. While solar lamps are extensively illustrated in these trade publications, Argand and sinumbra lamps are not.

The question has arisen as to whether or not lighting catalogues from the period 1800-1840 actually existed. Logic, as well as business correspondence with firms, dictates that such publications must have been employed, even if in limited numbers. From a practical point of view it would be difficult for companies the size of Messenger and Phipson (100-250 workers) and Cornelius to have attained such prominence without having pictorial examples of their wares. What might have happened to these documents is anyone's guess. The author maintains an optimistic attitude that in the future some of these works will surface and from their pages the Argands and sinumbras shall live again.

Values

The values given in this book are estimates and should serve strictly as a guide. There are many variables that determine each piece's value; these include condition, originality, extent of restoration, geography, rarity, desirability, and context of the sale. The lamps featured herein generally contain an intact and complete burner apparatus.

Values listed are what is believed to be reasonable for either a lamp restored to burn its intended fuel or electrified with preservation of as much of the burner elements as is practically possible and no unnecessary drilling of metal parts. Surface restoration was also considered.

Argand, sinumbra, and solar lamps, when initially produced, were fitted with wheel etched and hand cut blown glass shades, also referred to as First Period shades. Since few of these of globes survived, mass produced reproductions are common. The value of the lighting device so fitted is reduced accordingly.

The author fully acknowledges the variability of assigning a value to any antique including the lamps featured in this book. The designated values are the opinions of experts consulted by the author and may be somewhat arbitrary.

With respect to a lighting device's originality, Heinz Baumann perhaps best expresses the concept:

> The attribution of a given lamp as being in its original condition is difficult because most of the lamps are unmarked, consist of metal and glass parts that are interchangeable and have been subjected to modification during the many intervening years since their production.
>
> Contemporary descriptions, including catalogs of manufacturers and retail shops, are scarce and often not accessible[1].

The author and Publishing Company are not responsible if financial losses are incurred.

The Burning Burner Controversy

The President's Note, in the winter 2001 edition of *Flickerings*, a publication of The Rushlight Club, was devoted to the subject: "Do you collect the burner or the lamp?" That article describes two basic types of lighting collectors: those attracted to the aesthetics and those absorbed with technology. The President goes on to say that both groups can make contributions to the understanding of historical lighting[2]. I believe this statement to be true and therefore fail to appreciate any significant merit to the controversy. One camp certainly is not superior to the other.

Lamps sold at auction or by decorators that are often missing some or all burner components realize as much or more as those traded privately between burner technologists. In fact, decorators would be as hard pressed to sell unelectrified, oily, messy lamps to the general public as they would electrified ones to the burner enthusiasts. Both sides need to show mutual respect to further advance historic lighting.

Perhaps in the near future this relatively meaningless debate will burn itself out.

[1]Heinz Baumann, *The Rushlight,* Southampton, N.Y., The Rushlight Club, Volume 61, No. 3, September, 1995, pg. 3239.

[2]Dan Mattausch, *Flickerings,* Washington, D.C., The Rushlight Club, Winter, 2001, pgs. 1-2.

Overview of Lighting Fuels and Lamp Styles

Types of Lighting Fuels

For the purposes of this text the following terminology is utilized.

Whale Oil

This oil is derived chiefly from the blubber (fat) of the whale. It is generally considered an inferior quality or coarse grade oil that produces considerable smoke and odor when ignited. By the 1840s the whaling industry was in decline, raising the price of whale oil beyond most consumers, and cheaper sources of lighting were developed.

Sperm Whale Oil

Sperm whale oil comes from the cavity in the head of a sperm whale and is of superior quality to ordinary whale oil. Sperm whale oil is viscous, expensive, and its use was relatively limited even in the upper echelons of society in North America. This oil is sometimes referred to spermaceti.

Colza

This is a vegetable oil of high quality extracted from the rapeseed, a member of the cabbage plant family. Like sperm whale oil, it was quite viscous and relatively expensive. This fuel was used primarily in Europe.

Both Argand and sinumbra lamps were fitted with burners designed to utilize the high grade, heavy oils such as colza and sperm whale oil.

Burning Fluid

Reportedly invented by John Porter of Boston in 1834, burning fluid is the distillation product of a mixture of turpentine, alcohol, and other elements. It is quite fluid, burns brilliantly without smoke or odor but, regrettably, is very explosive and dangerous to use. Despite its drawbacks, burning fluid was widely used for several years.

Camphene

This compound is purified oil of turpentine. A process for camphene production was developed by A. V. H. Webb of New York City in 1839. Webb also secured a patent at that time for a lamp specifically designed to burn camphene. Because the light produced from camphene did not compare in quality to burning fluid and due to the dangers associated with its use, camphene never achieved widespread popularity. It is suitable for use in an Argand burner.

Lard

Lard is made from leftover cooking grease, usually from the hog. Therefore, it was cheap and accessible to almost everyone. Its problems as a lamp fuel centered on its semi-solid consistency, making it difficult to utilize and requiring a special burner. In part, the solar burner evolved to accommodate the use of lard, thus bringing cheap and relatively safe lighting to the general populace as a substitute for burning fluid, camphene, and whale oils. Lard was in popular use from approximately the late 1830s to the late 1850s. Its decline relates to the discovery of kerosene.

Styles of Lamps

Argand Lamps

An Argand lamp describes a lighting device that is equipped with an Argand designed fuel reservoir system along with an Argand burner. Usually such lamps have a fuel reservoir (font) that is located above and to the side of the burner. The burner is fed fuel horizontally by gravity through an arm or arms that extend between the font and the burner (see Figure 1).

Opposite page: Figure 1. Typical single light Argand lamp. Note that the font (fuel reservoir) is above and off to the side of the burner to facilitate the gravity fed fuel system. Fuel flows from the font through the fuel feeder arm to the offset burner.

In 1784, Ami Argand invented a burner composed of a tubular wick secured between two metal tubes. The center tube was open at the bottom, allowing air from the base to enter. A burner so constructed delivered air to the inside and outside of the flame, resulting in a dramatic increase in the amount of illumination (more complete combustion). Thus was born the Argand burner (see Figures 2-6).

Argand lamps were designed to burn higher grade oils such as colza and sperm whale oil. There are single light and dual light Argand lamps in addition to wall brackets and chandeliers. The single and dual light lamps often came in pairs or sets of three for use on the fireplace mantel. In this regard they are occasionally referred to as mantel lamps or mantel-arm lamps. Argand lamps were most often constructed of bronze and/or brass. Occasionally a plating of silver was used and crystal varieties are found.

Figure 2: Typical Argand burner (glass shade and chimney removed) showing thimble-like wick holder at maximum elevation. The wick has been removed for better visualization of the burner. Argand burners consist of several components. The outer housing is called the burner tube. Within the burner tube is a central draft tube that is fixed in position and open at the bottom to allow for entry of air (better shown in Figures 3-6). Around the central draft tube is a wick raiser tube that is free to move up and down when it is engaged in the spiral groove on the outside of the central draft tube. The thimble-like wick holder fits inside the wick raiser tube and fastens to the base of the wick by means of tiny external "teeth." It moves in concert with the wick raiser tube by following the grooves in the central draft tube and raises and lowers the wick when the shade ring/chimney holder is rotated. Collectively, these burner elements comprise the so-called "spiral wick raiser mechanism."

Figure 3: Note how the chimney is held in place by the four prong cage and surrounding upwardly directed flange that are part of the shade holder. The chimney cage is sometimes referred to as a "spider." Argand himself made the observation that the addition of the chimney further enhanced the brightness of the flame.

Figure 4: Detail of an Argand burner showing all components except the wick holder and wick (glass shade and chimney removed).

Figure 5. Detail of the burner with all components removed except for the central draft tube which is permanently fixed into position within the burner tube.

Figure 6. Disassembled view of the burner components, including shade ring/chimney holder unit (top left), central draft tube position fixed within the burner tube (top right), wick raiser tube (bottom left) and thimble-like wick holder (bottom right).

Often, crystal pendants are suspended from rings found either on the font or on the burner shaft or in both locations. Most often American retailers requested these pendants, as they were popular in the United States during this period (see Figure 7).

Argand lamps were used from the late eighteenth century to the latter second quarter of the nineteenth century, at which time their popularity declined. A major shortcoming of these lamps was a shadow cast by the fuel reservoir. Another weakness was the cumbersome and messy refueling procedure that required removal of the font pendant ring (if present), unscrewing the font from the standard, and inverting it all before the fuel supply could be replenished (see Figure 8).

Argand lamps were reproduced in the last quarter of the nineteenth century, or the so called Second Period. Such reproductions are unlikely to have a burner of any type, a font designed to hold fuel, or a fuel adjustment lever (see Figures 9 and 10).

Figure 7. View of separate and distinct shade ring/chimney holder (gilt brass) and glass pendent ring. Be aware that in First Period Argand lamps the shade ring/chimney holder and pendant ring (if present) had to be separate components. If crystal pendants were attached to the shade ring/chimney holder, then when this device was rotated to adjust the wick, the pendants would impact against the fuel feeder arm. Today Argand lamps modified to include pendants hanging from the shade ring are commonly encountered. The reader should be aware that the location of such pendants indicates that they are a later addition.

Figure 8. Font removed from lamp shown in previous pictures. When refueling an Argand lamp, the font had to be so removed and inverted. Fuel was then added through the tube at the bottom of the font. Once the font was filled it had to be reattached to the main body of the lamp. Such a procedure was time consuming and messy.

Figure 9. Detail of the fuel valve adjustment lever found on all First Period Argand lamps. This lever is almost always located at the base of the font just above the standard, but may be occasionally found adjacent to the font finial. The lever mechanism controls the amount of fuel released from the font through the fuel feeder arm to the burner. In this example, the lever moves from side to side along a curved, slit-like aperture. Depending on the position of the lever, the aperture serves as a vent to facilitate fuel delivery. The letter "O" is stamped into the metal at the far right margin of the aperture to indicate the "off" position of the adjustment lever. Other Argand lamps may have the words "on" and "off" or "open" and "shut" stamped at opposite ends of the aperture. Still other Argand lamps with a different internal shut off mechanism have a fuel valve adjustment lever that moves up and down through a small circular aperture. In these lamps a circular vent is located directly opposite the adjustment lever. The fuel adjustment lever is often missing in First Period Argand lamps that have been electrified. Reproduction lamps do not have a fuel adjustment lever as their fonts are not designed to hold fuel.

Figure 10. Internal detail of the fuel adjustment lever and refueling tube, indicating that this font is intended to hold fuel.

Sinumbra Lamps

These lamps have a doughnut or ring shaped font with an Argand burner located in the center of the ring. The burner is set at font level to provide even delivery of the fuel through a gravity system with the use of two feeder tubes. The ring configuration of the font and central location of the burner allows illumination downward through the open space without casting a shadow, hence the Latin designation of "sine umbra" or "without shadow" (see Figures 11 and 12). Like Argand lamps, sinumbras were designed to burn the high grade, heavy oils. These lamps were intended to be mounted on a standard or suspended from the ceiling. Fonts were usually manufactured of tin with most standards made of brass and/or bronze. Rarely, glass was used to form the base or the standard.

The history of these lamps begins in France around 1806, where Count Rumford developed a lamp with a circular reservoir in the form of a hollow, flat ring on which the globe was supported. This was the forerunner of the sinumbra lamp. It was

Figure 11. Example of a First Period sinumbra lamp. Note the central location of the burner and *two* fuel feeder tubes extending between the font and the burner.

Figure 12. Sinumbra lamp font, fuel feeder tubes, and burner as viewed from above with glass globe removed. The sinumbra lamp is fitted with a typical Argand burner quite similar to that depicted earlier in this Overview (see above). In this example, note the central location of the burner within the ring shaped font and the two fuel feeder tubes. Sinumbra fonts were often painted white to aid in refection of light. Removing the fuel cap and adding heavy oil refuels the font, a much less cumbersome procedure than that used for Argand lamps. Rarely, one finds two fuel caps covering apertures that communicate with the inside of the font. These apertures are located 180 degrees apart, directly over the origins of the fuel feeder tubes. It has been postulated that in addition to refueling, two apertures facilitated venting and/or allowed stylet access to the fuel feeder tubes to assure patency.

mounted on a columnar stand and was for table use. Unfortunately, Rumford did not believe in patenting his inventions.

In 1809, Bordier-Marcet secured patents in France for "Lampe Astrale." The suspended version was patented in 1809 and the table model in 1810.

A further refinement of the "Astrale" lamp, designed to minimize the shadow cast by the ring font, was accomplished by thinning out the inner edge to make the font wedge shaped in cross section. Such a lamp was patented in France in 1820 by George Phillips of London and was known as the "Lampe Sinombra." Also in 1820, Samuel Parker in England obtained a patent for the same style lamp.

Nomenclature concerning these lamps may sometimes be confusing, particularly when referring to older literature. The term "astral" or "astrale," meaning "star-like," is often applied to sinumbra lamps and solar lamps. Consultation with several lighting experts produced considerable rhetoric and no consistent definition of "astral lamp." Therefore, to simplify the terminology, the author has elected to entirely omit the term "astral lamp" from this text.

The following statements are generally true concerning First Period English and American sinumbra lamps and may help the reader distinguish between later reproductions:

1) Crystal pendants suspended from the shade ring are usually a later addition although the lamp may be otherwise original.

2) The base (plinth) is rarely marble on First Period lamps.

3) First Period sinumbras utilize two fuel feeder tubes. If three or more feeder tubes are present, suspect a later reproduction, often a kerosene-burning lamp from the Colonial Revival Period, sometimes referred to as the Second Period.

4) First Period fonts are usually made of tin and rarely of pewter. A brass font implies a kerosene era reproduction.

By the early 1850s, these lamps began to lose favor and production was substantially reduced. To preserve the esthetics and use of these lamps, solar burners were often substituted for the original Argand burners.

Solar Lamps

Solar lamps (so called because their illumination was thought to be comparable to sunlight) are believed to have originated in England and came to widespread use after Jeremiah Bynner's draft deflector lamp patent issued in England on December 9, 1837. Furthermore, it appears that the solar lamp evolved as the end result of several improvements by different individuals in England and in the United States. Therefore, the lamp probably did not suddenly arise as a full-blown patented invention, leading to a diverse array of solar burners with distinct variations produced by different makers.

Figure 13 illustrates a typical solar lamp. The distinctive features of these lamps are in the burner. The general design is that of a typical central draft Argand burner with a spiral wick raiser. In addition, a deflector cap in the form of an inverted saucer with an aperture about the size of the wick sits over the wick. This deflector cap directs the external draft inward toward

Figure 13. Signed Cornelius and Company solar lamp illustrating the commonly encountered features of an inverted pear shaped font, columnar standard, and double marble base (plinth).

the burner, thus giving the flame more oxygen. The result of this burner modification produced a high, narrow, and intense flame comparable to that seen with sperm whale oil and colza while burning much cheaper types of fuel. Solar lamps were intended to burn the inferior grades of whale oil, lard, and olive oil. In North America they were used mainly with lard.

Figures 14-17 portray a typical solar burner manufactured by the Cornelius Company of Philadelphia. A different solar burner credited to another maker, probably from the Boston area, is shown in Figures 18-22.

Figure 14. Detail of font and external burner components from the lamp shown in Figure 13. Rotation of the shade ring raises and lowers the wick. In this example of a Cornelius solar burner, the deflector, which is not attached to the shade ring, holds the chimney in place.

Figure 15. Burner deflector and chimney removed as a unit from the lamp shown in Figure 13. Note how the solar chimney has an upward taper.

Figure 16. View of the disassembled burner deflector components. The chimney fastening ring (right) slips over the top of the chimney and screws onto the body of the deflector (left), thereby holding the chimney flange in place.

Figure 17. Detail of previously seen lamp's internal burner mechanism, illustrating the font with wick raiser tube, central draft tube, and wick located between the two. Note that when a solar burner is referred to as "3/4 inch," as in this case, the measurement describes the diameter of the central draft tube. Further observe that the wick raiser tube and central draft tube extend to the bottom of the font. So positioned these burner components would be immersed in the fuel filling the font. Some heat from the flame is transmitted downward through these metal tubes, which facilitated keeping the fuel (lard) in a liquid state. As mentioned, the deflector components are not attached to the shade ring and can be removed from the burner as a unit (see Figures 15 and 16), leaving the shade ring in place. With the removal of the deflector, the lamp may then be refueled.

Figure 20. Detail of the top of the font from the lamp in Figure 18. In this view, the shade ring/burner deflector is removed, exposing the two apertures that engage the wick raiser pegs. The metal disc containing the two apertures is affixed to the top of the wick raiser tube.

Figure 18. Solar lamp showing a somewhat different and less sophisticated burner mechanism than that manufactured by Cornelius. This burner construction is attributable to several different Boston lighting firms. As in the previous example, the wick is raised and lowered by rotating the shade ring.

Figure 21. Further disassembly of the burner exposes the 9/16" central draft tube and surrounding wick.

Figure 19. In this lamp the burner deflector and shade ring (shown in the inverted position) are a one-piece unit. Note the two wick raiser pegs on the underside of the deflector. These pegs engage the two apertures present in the metal disc surrounding the burner that is attached to the top of the wick raiser tube.

Figure 22. Disassembled burner components showing font with central draft tube and outer wick (left), wick raiser tube (center), one-piece shade ring/burner deflector (right), and chimney fastening ring (bottom). Not shown is the metal wick holder, a small thimble-like device located at the base of the wick.

When citing the lighting catalogues in Chapters One and Two, the Hooper Company mentions solar burners of 3/4" and 9/16" as well as occasional other sizes. These measurements refer to the diameter of the solar burner's central draft tube. All other factors being equal, the larger the central draft tube the more light produced. The author's research indicates that in the Starr, Fellows catalogue a 3/4" burner is referred to as a No. 1 and a 9/16" burner as a No. 2. Other manufacturers have similar sized solar burners.

Unfortunately, today it is rare to find a solar lamp with a complete and intact original burner. Identification now rests with the shape of the font and any burner remnants available.

Solar lamps usually have an inverted pear shaped font. The font may be mounted on a standard, hung on the wall, suspended from the ceiling, or in the form of a chandelier.

These lamps were manufactured using a variety of materials, primarily brass and bronze. Occasional standards are made of cut glass.

The solar chimney is unique in shape, being cylindrical with a slightly upward taper and a flange at the base that engages the collar of the deflector cap which holds it in place.

By the early 1840s, these lamps were in general use in the United States. Their popularity waned in the late 1850s with the increasing use of cheaper and more efficient kerosene.

Today, if one wishes to burn an Argand, sinumbra, or solar lamp, mineral oil will suffice as a fuel.

Nineteenth Century Lighting Device Manufacturers

Chapter One

Henry N. Hooper & Company

Henry Northey Hooper (1799-1865) of Boston, Massachusetts was already winning awards for metal work in 1817 at the age of eighteen years. He won a gold medal for his exhibit of lamps listed in the catalogue of the Massachusetts Mechanics' Association First Exhibition and Fair.

Hooper is first listed in the Boston City Directory in 1823 as a mathematical instrument maker; the address is Drawbridge 43 Ann.

The 1828 city directory finds Hooper a Boston Copper Company agent and two years later he is described as a "successor" to the late Company.

In 1832, he formed a partnership with William Blake and Thomas Richardson, known as Henry N. Hooper and Company. The firm specialized in metal castings and offered a wide variety of lighting devices, including Argand and sinumbra lamps and later solar lamps and gasoliers.

In 1850 and again in 1858, the company published trade catalogues illustrating its lighting wares. The author knows of three of these catalogues that survive today. A private collector owns both an original 1850 and 1858 Hooper catalogue. Another 1858 Hooper catalogue can be found in the Peabody Essex Institute in Salem, Massachusetts.

In this chapter, the only known 1850 Hooper trade catalogue is reproduced in its entirety. This approximately 60-page document contains invaluable information concerning lighting styles, terminology, measurements, etc. for the period. Obviously, many of the company's metal castings are interchangeable, allowing for manipulation of components to satisfy the customers' needs. As the catalogue states: "Executed to Order" and "as may be wanted."

Numerous catalogue illustrations depict standards, pedestals, bases, and plinths for use on either solar or sinumbra lamps as well as some Argands. By the time of the catalogue's publication, most lamps had gone "solar," therefore specific examples of Argand and sinumbra lighting are not found. However, it is easy to imagine certain standards supporting ring shaped fonts and/or Argand fuel reservoirs from an earlier time period.

Meticulous review of both the 1850 and 1858 catalogues reveals only trivial differences between the two documents. The print styles on the introductory pages are slightly different. By 1858, the firm's retail store had relocated from 58 to 24 Commercial Street in Boston. All item numbers remain identical for both catalogues.

With Hooper's death in 1865 the business declined and closed its doors three years later.

Hooper lighting products often but not always exhibit the maker's mark. Argand, sinumbra, and solar lamps may show "H N Hooper & Co Boston," sometimes with an accompanying number stamped on the cast iron base weight. On both Argand and sinumbra lamps, a brass plate bearing the company's name is often affixed to the burner tube. Solar burners may be marked on the deflector: "Hooper & Co Boston Solar" or "H N Hooper Boston." Today, Hooper solar lamps are particularly difficult to identify because so few retain their original burner elements where the manufacturer's mark was typically located.

The following pages depict the 1850 Hooper catalogue in its entirety, followed by many examples of the company's lighting wares.

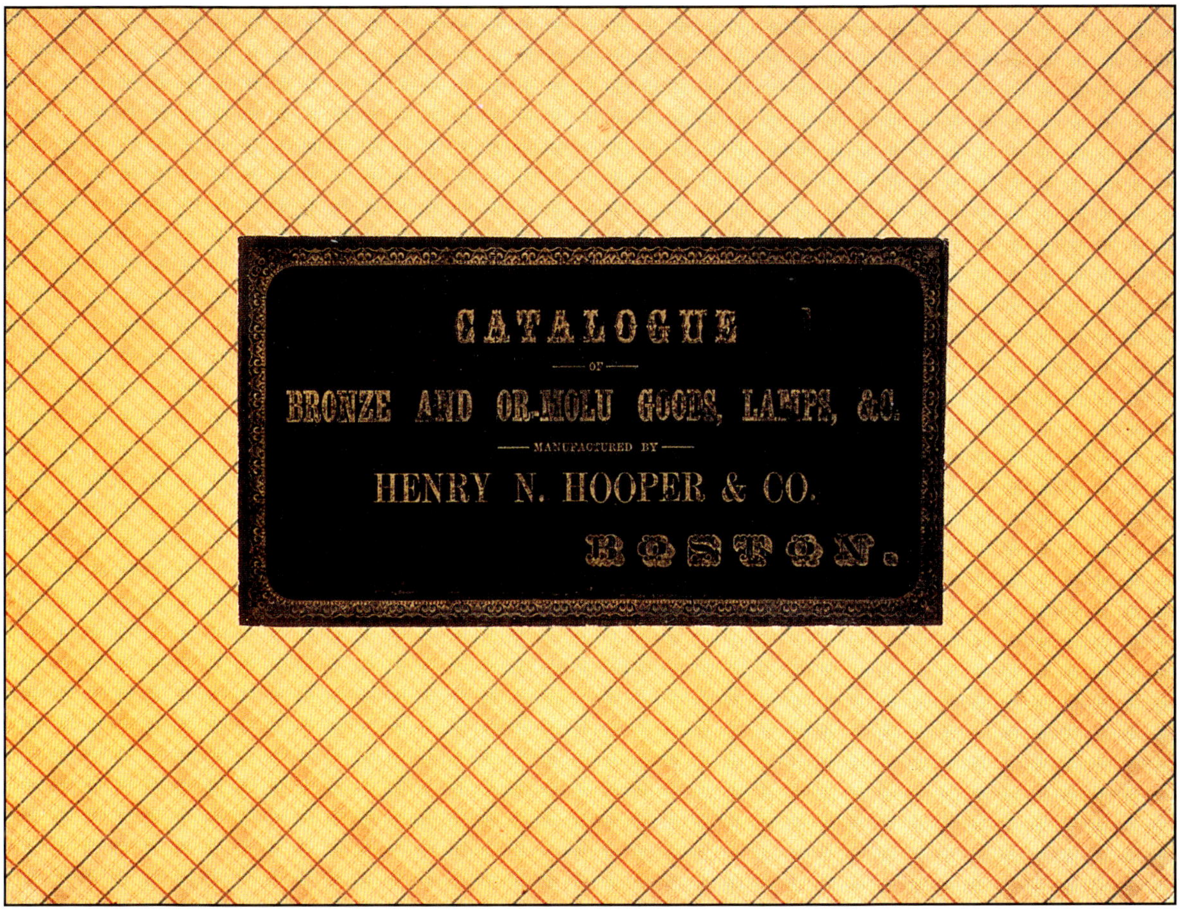

Front cover of the original 1850 Henry N. Hooper and Company Trade Catalogue (Boston, Massachusetts).

HENRY N. HOOPER & CO.

COPPER DEALERS, FOUNDERS, AND MANUFACTURERS,

ARE PREPARED TO SUPPLY

MERCHANTS AND SHIP BUILDERS

WITH SHEATHING COPPER AND YELLOW METAL, COPPER AND YELLOW METAL BOLTS, CAST COMPOSITION SPIKES, WOOD-END AND BUTT BOLTS, CLINCH RINGS, RUDDER JOINTS, COPPER AND WOOD SHEATHING NAILS, BRASS RINGS, TOPS AND PALL BEDS FOR VESSELS CAPSTANS, IN EVERY VARIETY AND SIZE WHICH MAY BE REQUIRED

ALSO, HAVE JUST INTRODUCED

MACHINE-WROUGHT YELLOW METAL SPIKES,

A NEW ARTICLE FOR VESSELS, AND POSSESSING ADVANTAGES OVER THE ORDINARY CAST SPIKES.

CASTINGS

OF EVERY KIND, IN COPPER, COMPOSITION, BRASS AND GERMAN SILVER, EXECUTED TO ORDER.

BELLS.

Church Bells in Setts, correctly tuned, or single, of any size required. Bells for Factories, Ships, or Railroads, plain or polished, of all sizes.

LOCOMOTIVE LANTERNS.

LANTERNS CONSTRUCTED EXPRESSLY FOR LOCOMOTIVE ENGINES, WITH SUPERIOR REFLECTORS.

Chandeliers, Girandoles, Candelabra, and Lamps,

In great variety of patterns, and of the most approved styles, for GAS, OIL and CANDLES, finished in Plain, Olive and Antique Bronze, Ormolu, or Gold and Silver Plate, as may be wanted.—Great care has been taken to bring this branch of business to a high state of perfection, and no pains spared to insure a thorough finish in every particular.

LIGHT-HOUSE WORK.

Lighting Apparatus of the best description. Our Reflectors are formed on dies of true parabola, and every portion of the work constructed to insure the greatest durability.

FACTORY, CAUSEWAY STREET. | BOSTON, 1850. | HENRY N. HOOPER, WILLIAM BLAKE, THOS. RICHARDSON. | BOSTON, 1850. | STORE, 24 COMMERCIAL STREET.

Descriptive page of the different wares produced by the Hooper Manufacturing Company.

DESCRIPTIVE CATALOGUE.

Number			$	cts.
Number	1	Solar Stand Lamp, 3-4 inch burner,		
"	2	" " " " " "		
"	14	" " " " " "		
"	26	" " " " " "		
"	28	" " " " " "		
"	40	" " " " " "		
"	43	" " " " " "		
"	48	" " " " " "		
"	71	" " " " " "		
"	72	" " " " " "		
"	77	" " " " " "		
"	80	" " " " " "		
"	81	" " " " " "		
"	83	" " " " " "		
"	85	" " " " " "		
"	86	" " " " " "		
"	97	" " " " " "		
"	102	Brass Study Lamp, 3-4 inch Argand burner,		
"	111	Tin " " " " " "		
"	112	Solar Stand " " " burner,		
"	118	Hall Lantern, for oil or gas,		
"	134	Solar Stand Lamp, 3-4 inch burner,		
"	138	" " " " " "		
"	149	Hall Lantern,		
"	150	Brass Study Lamp, 2 light, 3-4 inch Argand burner,		
"	152	Solar Stand Lamp, 3-4 inch burner,		
"	161	" " " " " "		
"	178	" " " " " "		
"	179	" " " " " "		
"	191	Hall Lantern, for oil or gas,		
"	205	Solar Stand Lamp, 3-4 inch burner,		

Number			
Number	227	Solar Stand Lamp, 3-4 inch burner,	
"	251	Candlestick, cast flat bottom,	
"	266	Girandole, 5 light,	
"	267	" 3 "	
"	268	Girandole, 2 or 3 light,	
"	273	" 1 light,	
"	274	" 3 "	
"	278	Pulpit Stand Solar Lamp, 3-4 inch burner,	
"	285	Hanging Girandole, 5 light,	
"	312	Girandole, 1 light,	
"	316	" 1 "	
"	318	" 3 "	
"	322	" 5 "	
"	324	Solar Stand Lamp, 3-4 inch burner,	
"	328	Girandole, 3 light,	
"	329	Solar Stand Lamp, 3-4 inch burner,	
"	330	Girandole, 3 light,	
"	331	Solar Stand Lamp, 3-4 inch burner,	
"	332	Solar Hanging " " " "	Grecian Chain. Cheap do. do.
"	334	Girandole, 3 light,	
"	336	Solar Stand Lamp, 3-4 inch burner,	
"	337	" " " 9-16 " "	
"	338	" " " 3-4 " "	
"	343	Girandole, 1 light,	
"	344	" 3 "	
"	346	Solar Stand Lamp, 3-4 inch burner,	
"	347	" " " " " "	
"	348	Girandole, 3 light,	
"	349	Solar Stand Lamp, 3-4 inch burner,	
"	350	Girandole, 2 light,	
"	351	" 3 "	

Page Number 1 of Descriptive Catalogue.

DESCRIPTIVE CATALOGUE.

Number			$	cts.
Number	352	Girandole, 3 light,		
"	355	" 2 "		
"	356	Hanging Candelabra, 5 light,		
"	357	Girandole, 3 light,		
"	359	Solar Bracket Lamp, 3-4 inch burner,		
"	360	Solar Chandelier, 2 light, 3-4 inch burner,		
"	361	" " 3 " " " "		
"	362	" " 4 " " " "		
"	364	Girandole, 2 light,		
"	365	" 1 "		
"	366	" 1 "		
"	367	" 2 or 3 light,		
"	370	Ship Solar Lamp, 3-4 inch burner,		
"	372	Candle Chandelier, 12 light, lustre,		
"	375	Solar Bracket Lamp, 3-4 inch burner,		
"	376	" " " " " "		
"	377	Girandole, 3 light,		
"	378	" 3 "		
"	381	" 1 " Rose Boy pattern,		
"	382	" 3 " " " "		
"	383	Liverpool Solar Hanging Lamp, 3-4 inch burner,		
"	384	Solar Stand Lamp, 3-4 inch burner,		
"	386	" " " " " "		
"	387	" " " " " "		
"	388	" " " " " "		
"	390	" " " " " "		
"	391	Girandole, 3 light,		
"	392	Solar Stand Lamp, 3-4 inch burner,		
"	393	" " " " " "		
"	394	" " " " " "		
"	395	" " " " " "		

Number			$
Number	396	Solar Stand Lamp, 9-16 inch burner,	
"	397	Tin Solar Study Lamp, 3-4 inch burner,	
"	398	Jackson's Chemical Lamp, 3-4 inch burner,	
"	400	Tin Side Solar Lamp, " " " 5 inch reflector,	
"	402	Solar Stand Lamp, 3-4 inch burner,	
"	403	" " " 9-16 " "	
"	404	" " " 3-4 " "	
"	405	" " " " " "	
"	406	" " " " " "	
"	407	" " " 9-16 " "	
"	408	" " " " " "	
"	409	" Bracket " " " "	
"	410	" Stand " " " "	
"	411	" " " 3-4 " "	
"	412	" " " 9-16 " "	
"	413	Girandole, 5 light,	
"	414	" 1 "	
"	415	Solar Stand Lamp, 3-4 inch burner,	
"	417	" " " " " "	
"	418	" Bracket " " " "	
"	419	" Stand " 9-16 " "	
"	420	Girandole, 3 light, 2 Deer Patt.	
"	421	" 1 " 1 " "	
"	422	Solar Chandelier, 6 light, 3-4 inch burner,	
"	423	Girandole, 2 light,	
"	424	" 1 "	
"	425	Solar Stand Lamp, 9-16 inch burner,	
"	426	" " " " " "	
"	428	Girandole, 5 light,	
"	429	Tin Solar Study Lamp, 3-4 inch burner,	
"	431	Solar Hanging " " " "	

Page Number 2 of Descriptive Catalogue.

Page Number 3 of Descriptive Catalogue.

DESCRIPTIVE CATALOGUE.

Number			$	cts.
Number	432	Solar Stand Lamp, 9-16 inch burner,		
“	436	Solar Chandelier, 8 light, 3-4 inch burner,		
“	437	Girandole, 3 light,		
“	438	“ 1 “		
“	439	Solar 3-4 inch burner,		
“	440	Solar Stand Lamp, “ “ “		
“	441	Girandole, 2 light,		
“	443	“ 1 “		
“	444	Solar Stand Lamp, 3-4 inch burner,		
“	445	“ “ “ 9-16 “ “		
“	446	Girandole, 1 light,		
“	447	“ 3 “		
“	448	“ 1 “		
“	449	“ 3 “		
“	450	Solar Hanging Lamp, 3-4 inch burner,		
“	451	“ Stand “ 9-16 “ “		
“	452	“ “ “ “ “ “		
“	453	Girandole, 3 light,		
“	454	“ 1 “		
“	455	Solar Stand Lamp, 3-4 inch burner, Tulip shaft,		
“	456	“ “ “ “ “ “		
“	457	Solar Chandelier, 2 light, 9-16 inch burner,		
“	“	“ “ 3 “ “ “ “		
“	“	“ “ 4 “ “ “ “		
“	458	Girandole, 5 light,		
“	459	Solar Stand Lamp, 3-4 inch burner,		
“	460	Girandole, 2 light,		
“	461	“ 3 “		
“	462	“ 3 “ Mastiff Dog pattern,		
“	463	“ 2 “ Scotch Hunter “		
“	464	“ 2 “ Smuggler “		

Number			$
Number	465	Girandole, 2 light,	
“	466	Solar Chandelier, 6 light, 3-4 inch burner,	
“	467	Solar Stand Lamp, “ “ “	
“	468	Girandole, 3 light,	
“	469	Solar Stand Lamp, 9-16 inch burner,	
“	470	“ “ “ 3-4 “ “	
“	471	Gas Chandelier, 4 light, Persian,	
“	“	“ “ 6 “ “	
“	472	“ “ 4 “ Sheet brass fit,	
“	473	“ “ 3 “ “ “ “	
“	474	“ “ 2 “ “ “ “	
“	475	“ “ 6 “ “ “ “	
“	476	“ “ 4 “ “ “ “	
“	477	“ “ 2 “ “ “ “	
“	478	“ “ 6 “ Lustre,	
“	479	“ “ 4 “ “	
“	480	Gas Wall Bracket, 1 light, Tulip branch,	
“	481	“ “ “ 2 “ “	
“	482	Girandole, 1 light,	
“	483	“ 3 “	
“	484	Gas Chandelier, 2 light,	
“	485	Solar Stand Lamp, 3-4 inch burner,	
“	486	“ “ “ “ “ “	
“	487	“ “ “ 9-16 “ “	
“	488	“ “ “ “ “ “	
“	489	Gas Chandelier, 6 light,	
“	490	Solar Stand Lamp, 9-16 inch burner,	
“	491	Girandole, 3 light,	
“	492	“ 5 “	
“	493	Solar Stand Lamp, 9-16 inch burner,	
“	494	Gas Chandelier, 3 light, Sheet brass fit,	

DESCRIPTIVE CATALOGUE.

Number			$	cts.
Number	495	Girandole, 5 light,		
“	496	Solar Stand Lamp, 3-4 inch burner,		
“	497	“ Bracket “ 9-16 “ “		
“	498	“ Hanging “ 3-4 “ “		
“	499	“ Stand “ “ “ “		
“	500	“ “ “ “ “ “ Tripod,		
“	501	“ “ “ “ “ “ “		
“	502	“ “ “ “ “ “ “		
“	503	“ “ “ “ “ “		
“	504	“ “ “ “ “ “ Tripod,		
“	505	“ “ “ “ “ “ Figure,		
“	506	Solar Chandelier, 10 light, 3-4 inch burner,		
“	507	Girandole, 3 light,		
“	508	“ 1 “		
“	509	“ 5 “		
“	510	Gas Chandelier, 2 light, Gothic style,		
“	511	“ “ 4 “ “ “		
“	512	Solar “ 4 “ 3-4 inch burner,		
“	513	Bracket Candelabra, 5 light,		
“	514	Entry Lantern, for oil or gas,		
“	515	Solar Stand Lamp, 3-4 inch burner,		
“	516	Girandole, 3 light,		
“	517	“ 3 “		
“	518	Solar Stand Lamp, 3-4 inch burner,		
“	519	Girandole, 5 light,		
“	520	Entry Lantern, for oil or gas,		
“	521	Gas Chandelier, 3 light, Gothic,		
“	522	“ “ 4 “ Grecian,		
“	523	“ “ 6 “ “		
“	524	“ Bracket, 1 “		

Number			$
Number	526	Gas Bracket, 1 light, Tulip branch pattern,	
“	527	“ “ 1 “ Grecian branch pattern,	
“	528	“ “ 1 “ “ “ “	
“	529	“ “ 1 “ Long, slim pattern,	
“	530	“ Store Pendant, 2 light,	
“	531	“ Pendent Bracket, 2 light,	
“	532	“ Chandelier, 12 light, Masonic Temple,	
“	533	“ “ 8 “ Horticultural Hall,	
“	534	“ “ 8 “ Persian,	
“	535	“ “ 6 “ “	
“	537	Solar Stand Lamp, 3-4 inch burner,	
“	538	Girandole, 1 light,	
“	539	“ 3 “	
“	540	“ 3 “	
“	541	Candelabra, 6 light,	
“	542	“ 6 “	
“	543	“ 5 “ French style—Lewis XIV.	
“	544	Solar Chandelier, 3 light,	
“	545	“ “ 4 “	
“	546	“ “ 4 “	
“	547	Girandole, 5 light,	
“	548	Gas Chandelier, 3 light, Tulip Tt.	
“	549	“ Bracket, 1 “ Gothic,	
“	550	Solar Chandelier, 4 “ Tulip Tt.	
“	551	Gas “ 4 “ “ “	
“	552	Solar “ 4 “ Lustre,	
“	553	“ “ 6 “ “	
“	554	Gas “ 6 “ Gothic,	
“	555	Solar “ 3 “ Tulip,	
“	556	Gas “ 2 “ “	

Page Number 4 of Descriptive Catalogue

DESCRIPTIVE CATALOGUE.

Number			$	cts.
Number	558	Gas Chandelier, 6 light, Tulip,		
“	560	Girandole, 3 light, Tripod,		
“	561	Solar Study Lamp, 9-16 inch burner,		
“	562	Gas Bracket, 1 light, Face, Wheat,		
“	563	Solar Stand Lamp, 9-16 inch burner,		
“	564	“ Chandelier, 4 light, Persian pattern,		
“	565	“ “ 3 “ “ “		
“	566	“ “ 2 “ Tulip Ft. “		
“	567	Gas Lustre “ 4 “		
“	568	Solar Stand Lamp, 3-4 inch burner,		
“	569	Girandole, 3 light,		
“	570	Solar Chandelier, 6 light,		
“	571	“ “ 4 “ Gothic face suspending bracket,		
“	572	“ “ 6 “ Glass dish and fount,		
“	573	Gas “ 8 “ “ “ “ “		
“	574	Candelabra, 12 “ “ “ “ “		
“	575	Solar Stand Lamp, 9-16 inch burner,		
“	576	Girandole Mirror, 4 light, or Painting,		
“	577	Candelabra, 4 light, Tripod, for table,		
“	578	Wall Girandole, 4 light, Mirror or Painting,		
“	579	Solar Stand Lamp, 3-4 inch burner, Tripod,		
“	580	Girandole, 5 light,		
“	581	“ 3 “		
“	582	“ 3 “		
“	583	“ 2 “		
“	584	“ 1 “ Side Branch, for pianoforte,		
“	585	“ 1 “ Match 583 or 584,		
“	586	“ 5 “		
“	587	“ 3 “		
“	588	Solar Stand Lamp, 9-16 inch burner, Tulip shaft,		
Number	590	Solar Stand Lamp, 3-4 inch burner,		
“	591	“ “ “ 9-16 “ “		
“	592	Girandole Mirror, 6 light, or Painting,		
“	593	“ 1 light, Tripod,		
“	594	Gas Chandelier, 4 light, glass dish and fount,		
“	595	Girandole, 2 light,		
“	596	“ 4 “ Elizabethan Mirror or Painting,		
“	597	Solar Stand Lamp, 3-4 inch burner,		
“	598	“ Hanging “ “ “ “		
“	599	“ Stand “ “ “ “		
“	600	“ “ “ “ “ “ “		
“	601	“ “ “ “ “ “ “		
“	602	Candelabra Hanging Wall, 5 light,		
“	603	Gas Face Suspending Bracket, 4 light, Gothic,		
“	604	Ship Solar Lamp, 9-16 inch burner,		
“	605	Gas Chandelier, 3 light,		
“	606	“ “ 4 “		
“	607	Candelabra, 5 “		
“	608	Gas Chandelier, 5 “		
“	609	Solar “ 4 “ 3-4 inch burner, Tulip pattern,		
“	610	“ “ 6 “ “ “ “ “ “		
“	611	“ Stand Lamp, 3-4 inch burner, large Tripod,		
“	612	Gas Chandelier, 6 light, Tulip pattern,		
“	613	“ “ 2 “ “ “		
“	614	Gas Wall Bracket, 2 light,		
“	615	Girandole, 4 light, Mirror or Painting,		
“	616	Hall Lantern, for oil or gas, Arabesque,		
“	617	Candelabra Wall Hanging, 6 light,		
“	618	Bracket Wall, for candles,		
“	619	Solar Stand Lamp, 9-16 inch burner, double marbles,		

Page Number 5 of Descriptive Catalogue.

DESCRIPTIVE CATALOGUE.

Number			$	cts.
Number	621	Solar Stand Lamp, 3-4 inch burner, double marbles,		
“	622	“ “ “ 9-16 “ “ “ “		
“	623	“ “ “ “ “ “ “ “		
“	624	“ “ “ 3-4 “ “ “ “		
“	625	“ “ “ “ “ “ “ “		
“	626	Bracket Mirror, 3 light, for wall,		
“	627	Solar Stand Lamp, 9-16 inch burner, double marbles,		
“	628	Bracket Wall Mirror, 6 light,		
“	629	Solar Chandelier, 3 light, 3-4 inch burner, Tulip,		
“	630	“ Hanging Astral Desk Lamp, 3-4 inch burner, with shade,		
“	631	“ Stand Lamp, 9-16 inch burner, double marbles,		
“	632	“ “ “ 3-4 “ “ “ “		
“	633	“ “ “ 3-4 “ “ “ “		
“	634	Girandole Mirror, 5 light,		
“	635	“ “ 3 “		
“	636	Solar Stand Lamp, 3-4 inch burner,		
“	637	Girandole Mirror, 4 light, or Painting,		
“	638	“ “ 4 “ “ Wall,		
“	639	Gas Bracket, 1 light, Lilly pattern,		
“	640	Gas Chandelier, 6 light, Arabesque,		
“	641	Candelabra, 6 light, Hanging,		
“	642	Gas Chandelier, 8 light, Arabesque,		
“	643	“ “ 4 “ “		
“	644	Girandole, 3 light, match No. 519,		
“	645	Candelabra, 7 light, stand of No. 579,		
“	646	Solar Chandelier, 4 light, 3-4 inch burner,		
“	647	“ “ 4 “ “ “ “		
“	648	“ “ 4 “ “ “ “ Gothic,		
“	649	“ “ 6 “ “ “ “ Tulip,		
“	650	Gas “ 4 “ Arabesque,		
Number	652	Girandole, 5 light, Grape branch,		
“	653	Solar Chandelier, 4 light, 3-4 inch burner, Tulip,		
“	654	Girandole, 3 light, Match to 652,		
“	655	“ 5 “ Elizabethan,		
“	656	“ 3 “ Tripod base,		
“	657	Gas Chandelier, 2 light,		
“	658	Solar Chandelier, 2 light, 3-4 inch burner, Arabesque,		
“	659	Girandole, 3 light, Harp pattern,		
“	660	Solar Stand Lamp, 3-4 inch burner,		
“	661	Gas Chandelier, 4 light, Lustre,		
“	662	Solar Bracket, 2 light, 3-4 inch burner,		
“	663	“ “ 1 “ “ “ “		
“	664	Girandole, 5 light, Elizabethan pattern,		
“	665	“ “ 1 “ Romeo and Juliet pattern,		
“	666	“ 3 “ “ “ “		
“	667	“ 3 “ Vase “		
“	668	“ 2 “ Antique “		
“	669	Gas Chandelier, 6 light, Arabesque Centre pattern,		
“	670	“ Girandole, 3 “		
“	671	“ Chandelier, 4 “ Arabesque Centre pattern,		
“	672	“ “ 3 “ Glass dish and fount,		
“	673	“ “ 1 “ “ “ “ “		
“	674	“ S Pendant, 1 light, or oval Pendant,		
“	675	Candelabra, 5 light,		
“	676	“ 6 “ glass dish and fount,		
“	677	Solar Chandelier, 3 light, “ “ “ 9-16 inch burner,		
“	678	“ “ 4 “ “ “ “ “ “ “		
“	679	Gas Bracket, 1 light, “*folded tubing*,”		
“	680	“ Pendant, 2 light,		
“	681	“ Chandelier, 4 light, glass dish and fount,		

Page Number 6 of Descriptive Catalogue.

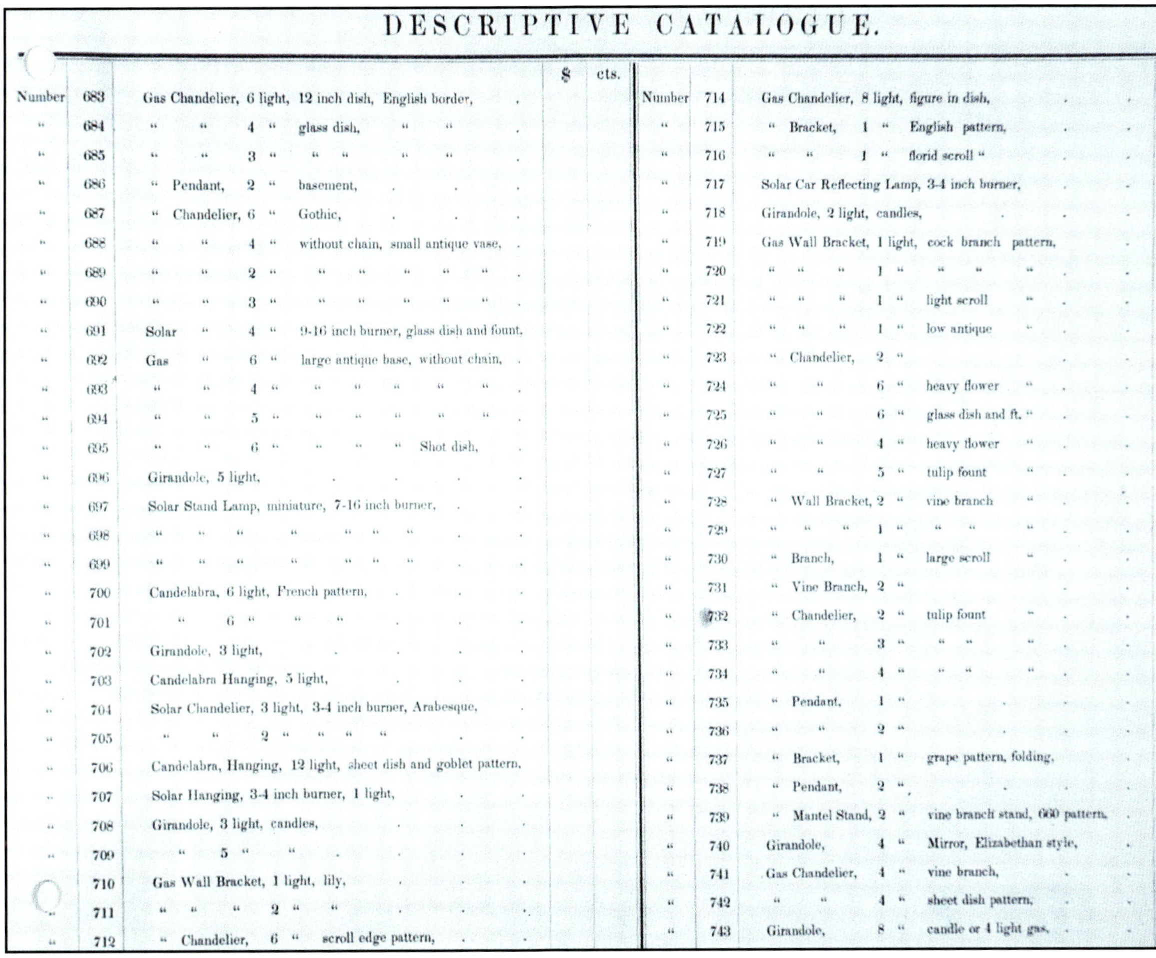

DESCRIPTIVE CATALOGUE.

			$	cts.
Number	683	Gas Chandelier, 6 light, 12 inch dish, English border,		
"	684	" " 4 " glass dish, " "		
"	685	" " 3 " " " " "		
"	686	" Pendant, 2 " basement,		
"	687	" Chandelier, 6 " Gothic,		
"	688	" " 4 " without chain, small antique vase,		
"	689	" " 2 " " " " " "		
"	690	" " 3 " " " " " "		
"	691	Solar " 4 " 9-16 inch burner, glass dish and fount,		
"	692	Gas " 6 " large antique base, without chain,		
"	693	" " 4 " " " " " "		
"	694	" " 5 " " " " " "		
"	695	" " 6 " " " " Shot dish,		
"	696	Girandole, 5 light,		
"	697	Solar Stand Lamp, miniature, 7-16 inch burner,		
"	698	" " " " " " "		
"	699	" " " " " " "		
"	700	Candelabra, 6 light, French pattern,		
"	701	" 6 " " "		
"	702	Girandole, 3 light,		
"	703	Candelabra Hanging, 5 light,		
"	704	Solar Chandelier, 3 light, 3-4 inch burner, Arabesque,		
"	705	" " 2 " " " "		
"	706	Candelabra, Hanging, 12 light, sheet dish and goblet pattern,		
"	707	Solar Hanging, 3-4 inch burner, 1 light,		
"	708	Girandole, 3 light, candles,		
"	709	" 5 " "		
	710	Gas Wall Bracket, 1 light, lily,		
	711	" " " 2 " "		
"	712	" Chandelier, 6 " scroll edge pattern,		

Number	714	Gas Chandelier, 8 light, figure in dish,
"	715	" Bracket, 1 " English pattern,
"	716	" " 1 " florid scroll "
"	717	Solar Car Reflecting Lamp, 3-4 inch burner,
"	718	Girandole, 2 light, candles,
"	719	Gas Wall Bracket, 1 light, cock branch pattern,
"	720	" " " 1 " " " "
"	721	" " " 1 " light scroll "
"	722	" " " 1 " low antique "
"	723	" Chandelier, 2 "
"	724	" " 6 " heavy flower "
"	725	" " 6 " glass dish and ft. "
"	726	" " 4 " heavy flower "
"	727	" " 5 " tulip fount "
"	728	" Wall Bracket, 2 " vine branch "
"	729	" " " 1 " " " "
"	730	" Branch, 1 " large scroll "
"	731	" Vine Branch, 2 "
"	732	" Chandelier, 2 " tulip fount "
"	733	" " 3 " " " "
"	734	" " 4 " " " "
"	735	" Pendant, 1 "
"	736	" " 2 "
"	737	" Bracket, 1 " grape pattern, folding,
"	738	" Pendant, 2 "
"	739	" Mantel Stand, 2 " vine branch stand, 660 pattern,
"	740	Girandole, 4 " Mirror, Elizabethan style,
"	741	Gas Chandelier, 4 " vine branch,
"	742	" " 4 " sheet dish pattern,
"	743	Girandole, 8 " candle or 4 light gas,

Page Number 7 of Descriptive Catalogue.

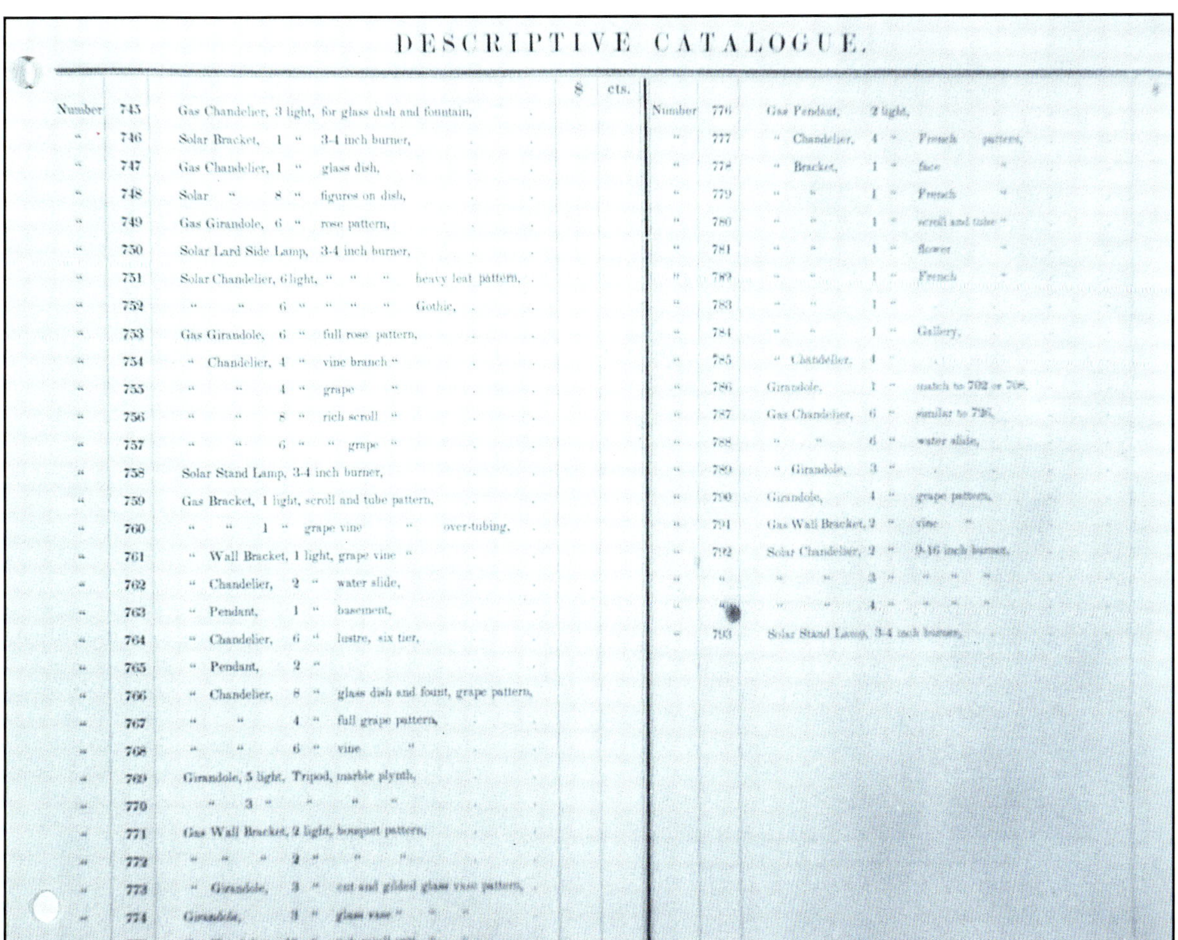

DESCRIPTIVE CATALOGUE.

			$	cts.
Number	745	Gas Chandelier, 3 light, for glass dish and fountain,		
"	746	Solar Bracket, 1 " 3-4 inch burner,		
"	747	Gas Chandelier, 1 " glass dish,		
"	748	Solar " 8 " figures on dish,		
"	749	Gas Girandole, 6 " rose pattern,		
"	750	Solar Lard Side Lamp, 3-4 inch burner,		
"	751	Solar Chandelier, 6 light, " " " heavy leaf pattern,		
"	752	" " 6 " " " " Gothic,		
"	753	Gas Girandole, 6 " full rose pattern,		
"	754	" Chandelier, 4 " vine branch "		
"	755	" " 4 " grape "		
"	756	" " 8 " rich scroll "		
"	757	" " 6 " " grape "		
"	758	Solar Stand Lamp, 3-4 inch burner,		
"	759	Gas Bracket, 1 light, scroll and tube pattern,		
"	760	" " 1 " grape vine " over-tubing,		
"	761	" Wall Bracket, 1 light, grape vine "		
"	762	" Chandelier, 2 " water slide,		
"	763	" Pendant, 1 " basement,		
"	764	" Chandelier, 6 " lustre, six tier,		
"	765	" Pendant, 2 "		
"	766	" Chandelier, 8 " glass dish and fount, grape pattern,		
"	767	" " 4 " full grape pattern,		
"	768	" " 6 " vine "		
"	769	Girandole, 5 light, Tripod, marble plynth,		
"	770	" 3 " " " "		
"	771	Gas Wall Bracket, 2 light, bouquet pattern,		
"	772	" " " 2 " " "		
"	773	" Girandole, 3 " cut and gilded glass vase pattern,		
"	774	Girandole, 3 " glass vase " " "		
"	775	Gas Chandelier, 10 " rich scroll patt. " "		

Number	776	Gas Pendant, 2 light,
"	777	" Chandelier, 4 " French pattern,
"	778	" Bracket, 1 " face "
"	779	" " 1 " French "
"	780	" " 1 " scroll and tube "
"	781	" " 1 " flower "
"	782	" " 1 " French "
"	783	" " 1 "
"	784	" " 1 " Gallery,
"	785	" Chandelier, 4 "
"	786	Girandole, 1 " match to 702 or 708,
"	787	Gas Chandelier, 6 " similar to 726,
"	788	" " 6 " water slide,
"	789	" Girandole, 3 "
"	790	Girandole, 4 " grape pattern,
"	791	Gas Wall Bracket, 2 " vine "
"	792	Solar Chandelier, 2 " 9-16 inch burner,
"	"	" " 3 " " " "
"	"	" " 4 " " " "
"	793	Solar Stand Lamp, 3-4 inch burner,

Page Number 8 of Descriptive Catalogue.

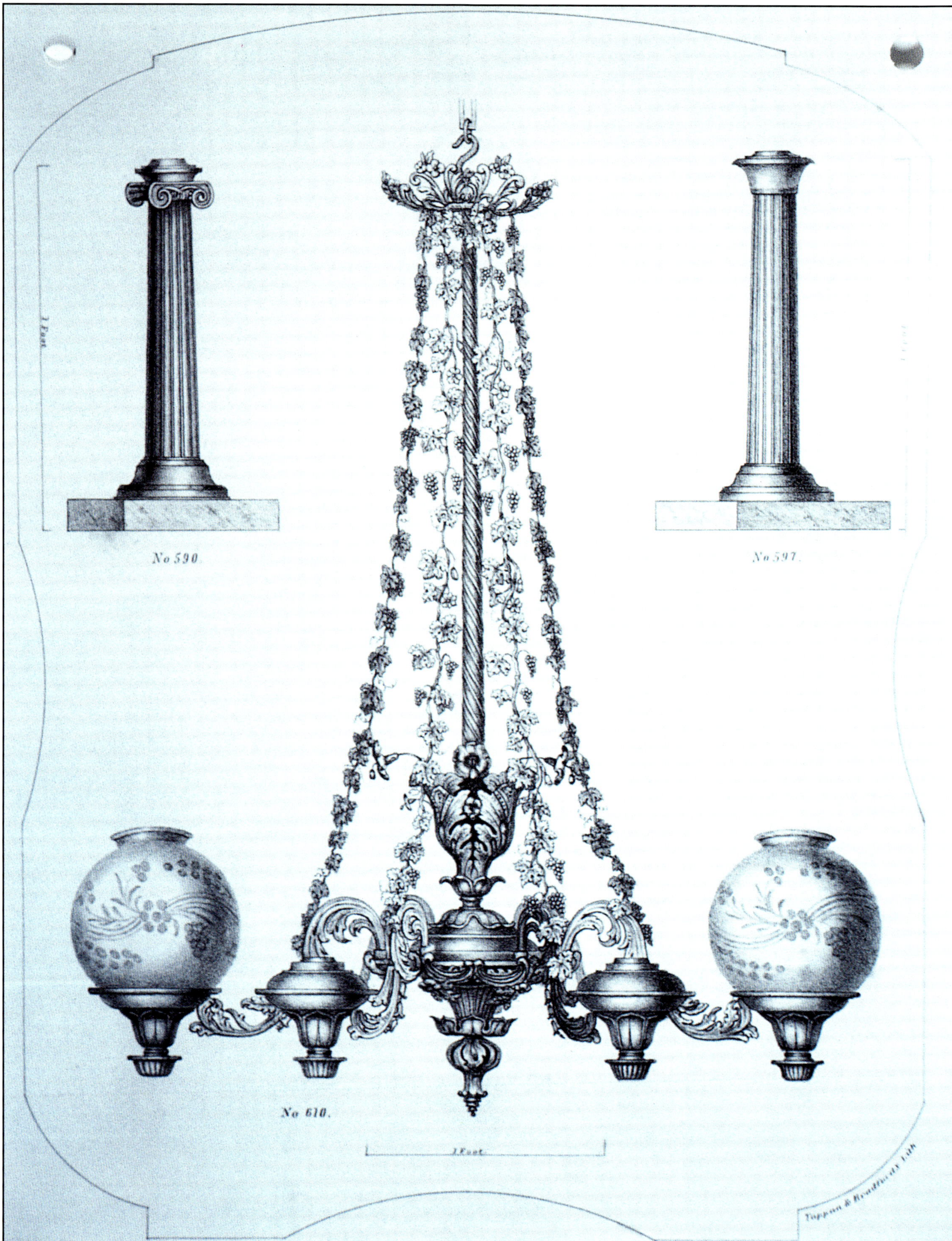

Clockwise from left: No. 590: solar stand lamp; No. 597: solar stand lamp; No. 610: solar chandelier.

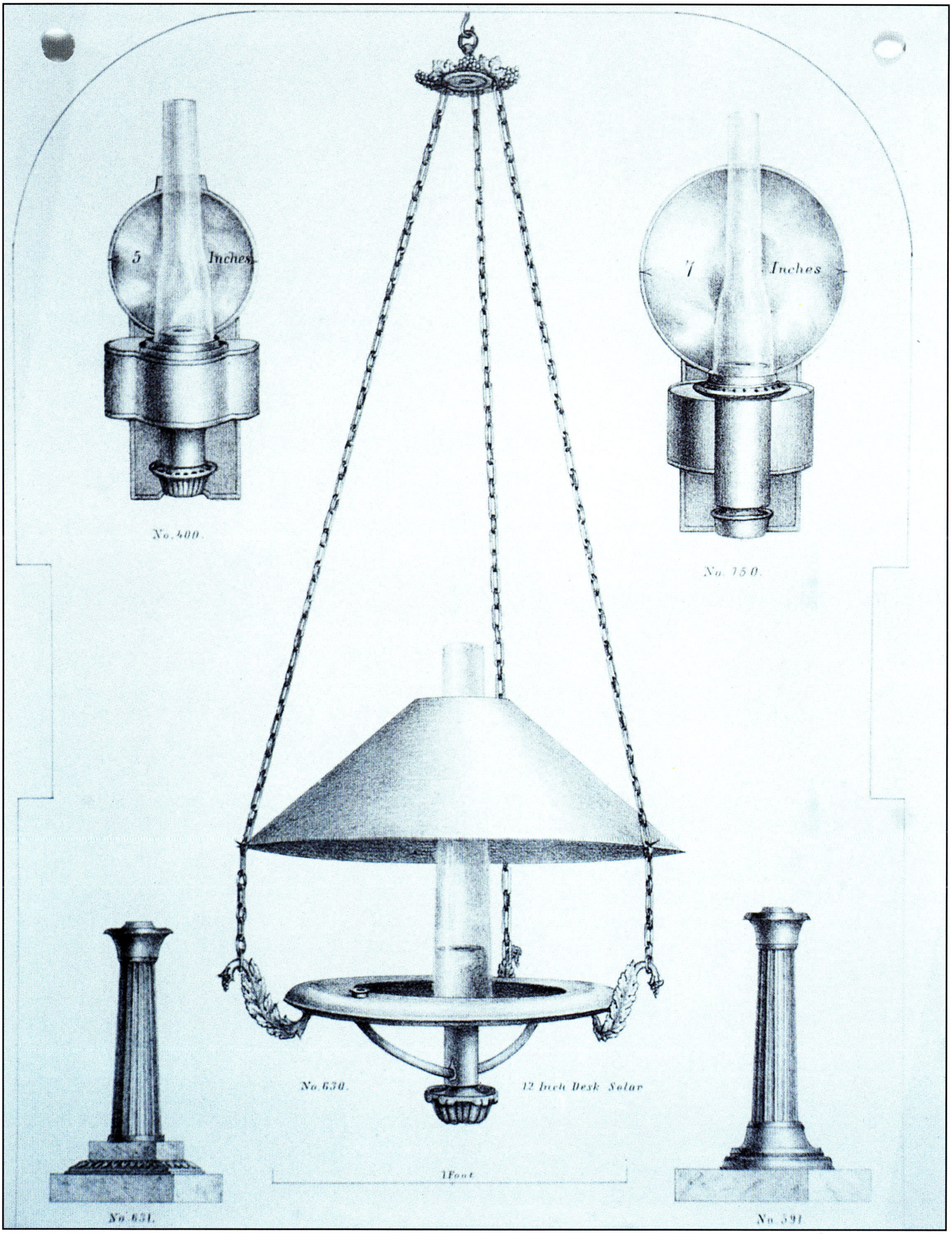

Clockwise from left: No. 400: tin side solar lamp; No. 750: solar lard side lamp; No. 591: solar stand lamp; No. 630: solar hanging astral desk lamp; No. 631: solar stand lamp.

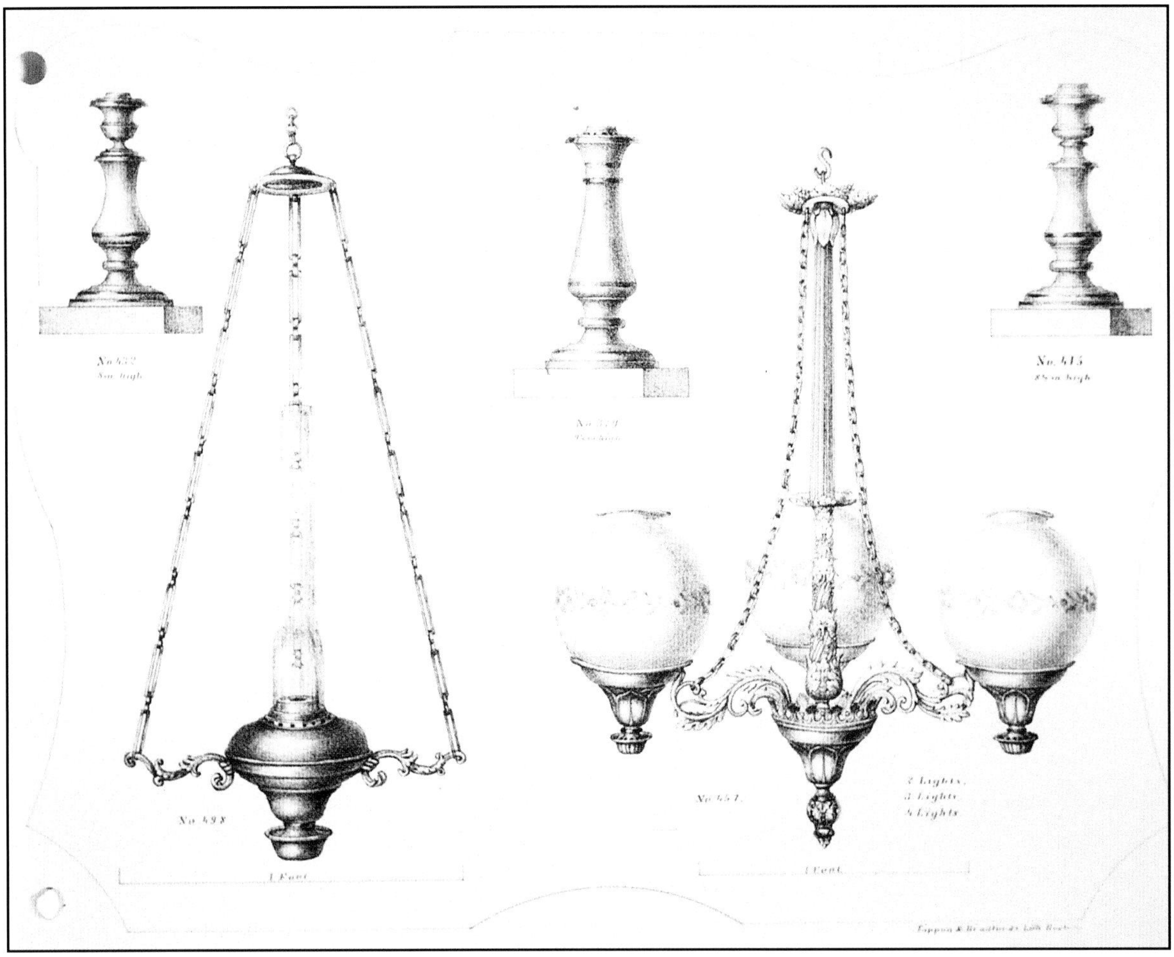

Top row, left to right: No. 432: solar stand lamp; No. 329: solar stand lamp; No. 415: solar stand lamp; Bottom row, left to right: No. 498: solar hanging lamp; No. 457: solar chandelier.

Top row, left to right: No. 501: solar stand lamp; No. 600: solar stand lamp; Bottom row, left to right: No. 336: solar stand lamp; No. 459: solar stand lamp; No. 388: solar stand lamp.

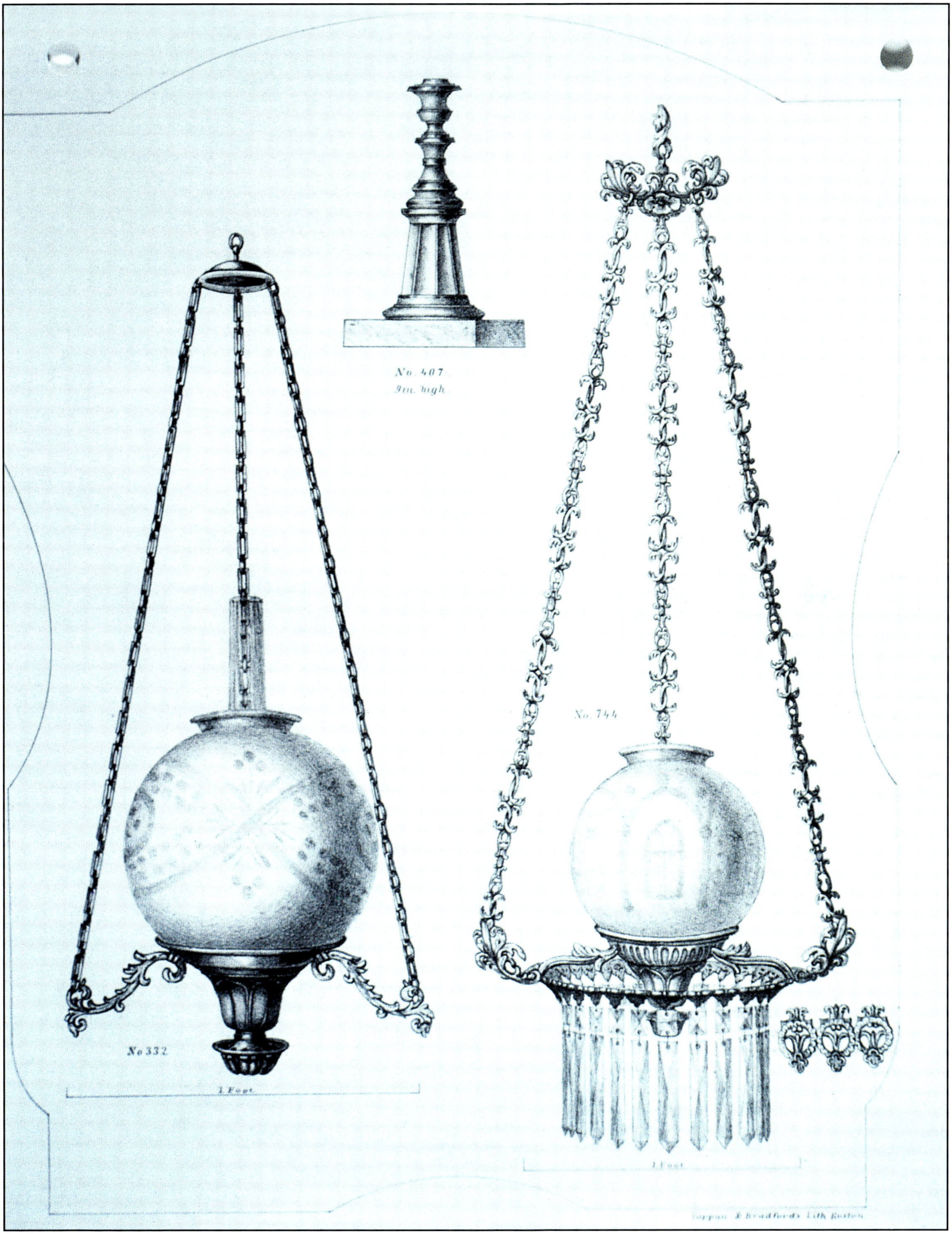

Top row: No. 407: solar stand lamp; Bottom row, left to right: No. 332: solar hanging lamp; No. 744: solar hanging lamp.

Top: No. 592: girandole mirror or painting; Bottom row, left to right: No. 438: girandole; No. 615: girandole mirror or painting.

Top row, left to right: No. 636: solar stand lamp; No. 336: solar stand lamp; No. 660: solar stand lamp;
Bottom row, left to right: No. 502: solar stand lamp; No. 579: solar stand lamp; No. 518: solar stand lamp.

Clockwise from left: No. 619: solar stand lamp; Nos. 586, 587: girandole; No. 665: girandole; No. 424: girandole; No. 581: girandole; boquet (sic) and glass (no number assigned).

Clockwise from left : Hand lamp (no number assigned); Nos. 702, 708: girandole; No. 699: solar stand lamp; eagle watch stand (no number assigned); Nos. 709, 696: girandole; snake watch stand (no number assigned).

Clockwise from left: No. 601: solar stand lamp; No. 318: girandole; No. 704: solar chandelier.

Clockwise from left: No. 419: solar stand lamp; No. 412: solar stand lamp; No. 451: solar stand lamp; No. 616: hall lantern; No. 425: solar stand lamp.

Top row, left to right: No. 460: girandole; No. 718: girandole; Bottom row, left to right: No. 585: girandole; Nos. 580, 581: girandole; No. 448: girandole.

Clockwise from left: No. 456: solar stand lamp; No. 423: girandole; No. 467: solar stand lamp; Nos. 152, 134, 227, 138: solar stand lamp; No. 458: girandole; Nos. 2, 77: solar stand lamp.

Clockwise from left: No. 493: solar stand lamp; Pianoforte stand (no number assigned); No. 627: solar stand lamp; No. 445: solar stand lamp; No. 519: girandole; No. 620: solar stand lamp.

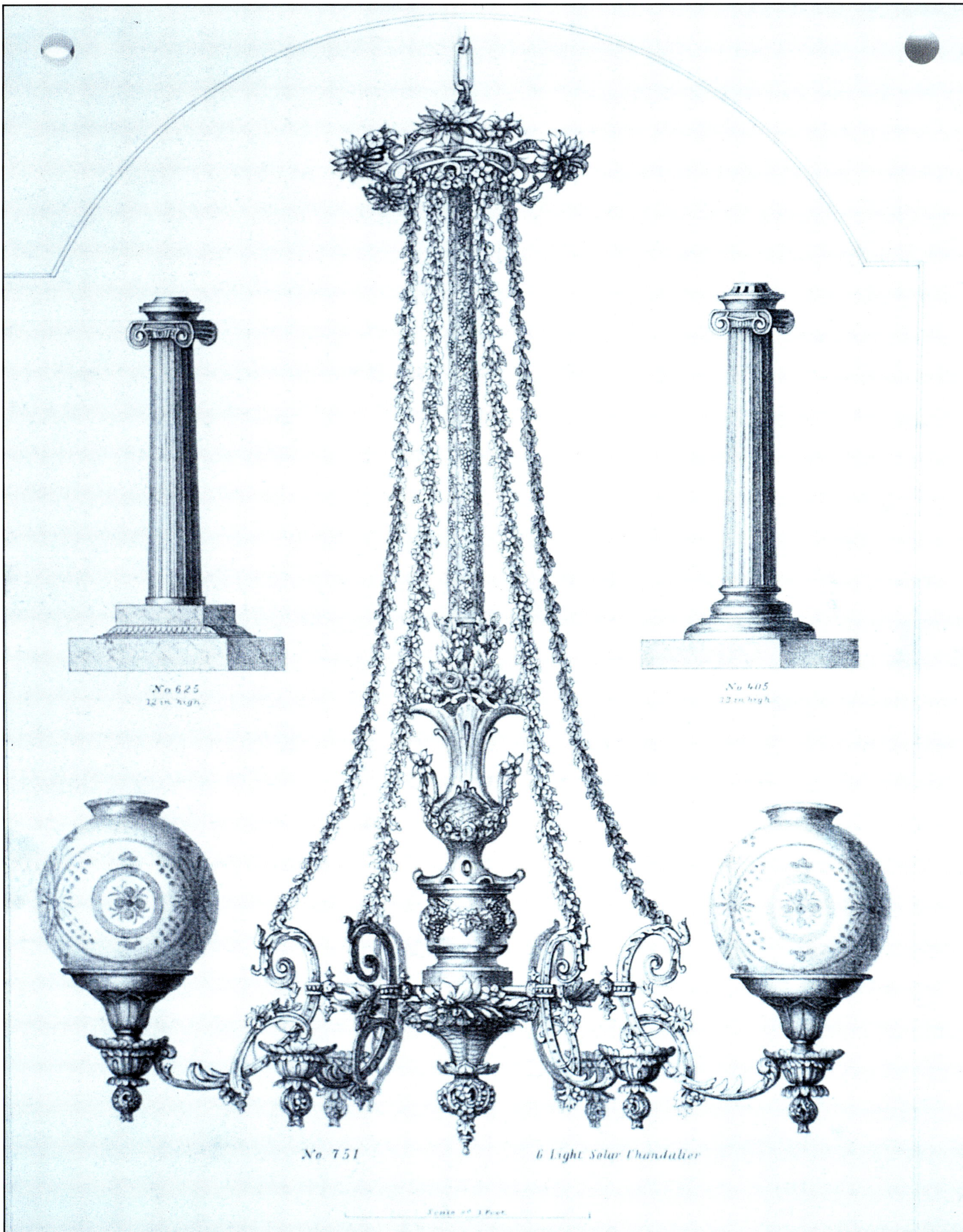

Clockwise from left: No. 625: solar stand lamp; No. 405: solar stand lamp; No. 751: solar chandelier.

Clockwise from left: No. 668: girandole; Nos. 463, 464: girandole; Nos. 582, 583: girandole; No. 449: girandole; middle, No. 593: girandole.

Clockwise from left: No. 418: solar bracket lamp; Nos. 376, 359: solar bracket lamp; No. 748: solar chandelier.

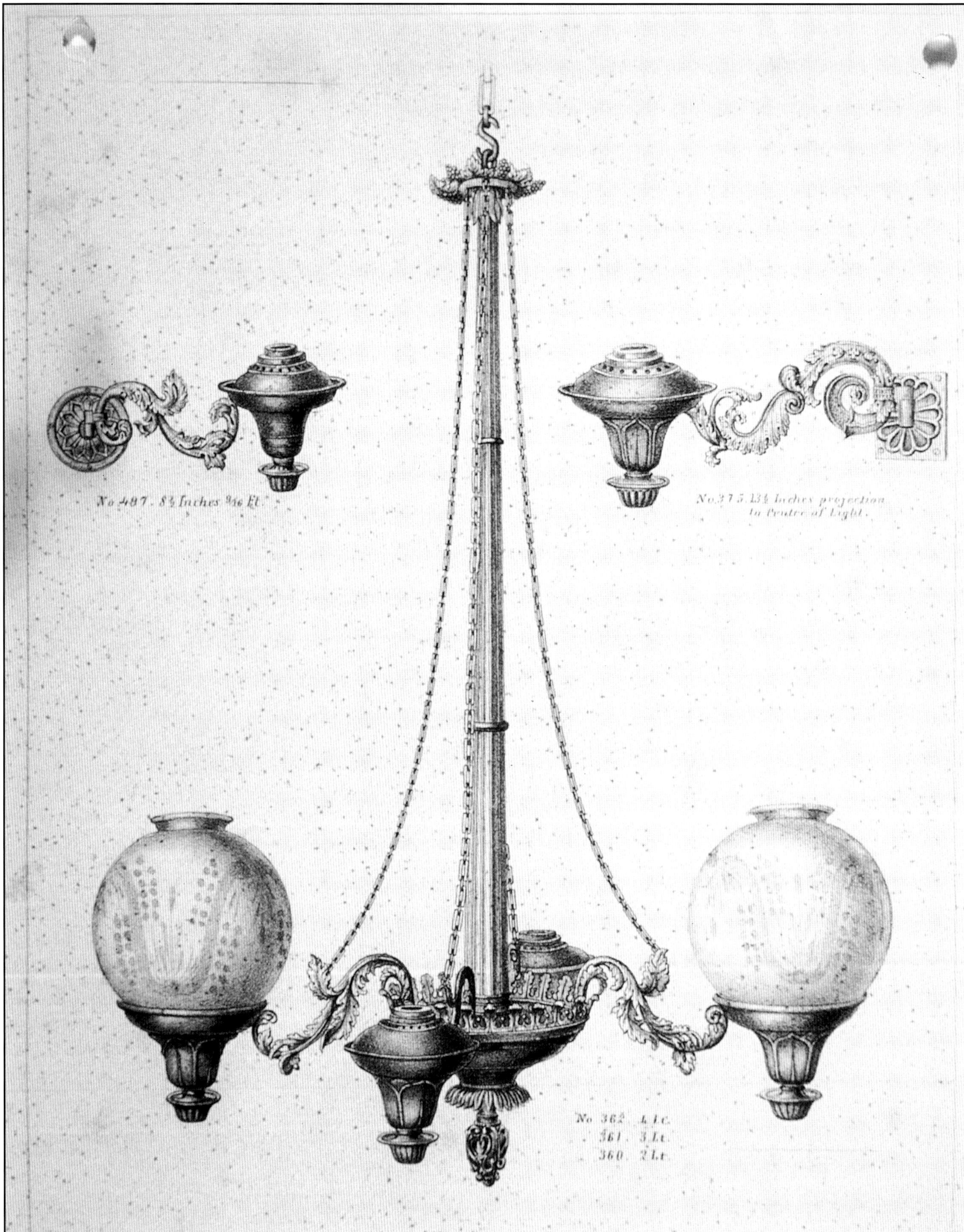

Clockwise from left: No. 497: solar bracket lamp; No. 375: solar bracket lamp; Nos. 362, 361, 360: solar chandelier.

Top row: Nos. 370, 604: ship solar lamp; No. 396: solar stand lamp; Nos. 662, 663: solar bracket lamp; Bottom row, left to right: No. 471: solar chandelier (this item is described as a "gas chandelier" in the Descriptive Catalogue); No. 351: girandole.

Left to right: No. 674: gas S pendant; No. 688: gas chandelier; No. 674: gas S pendant.

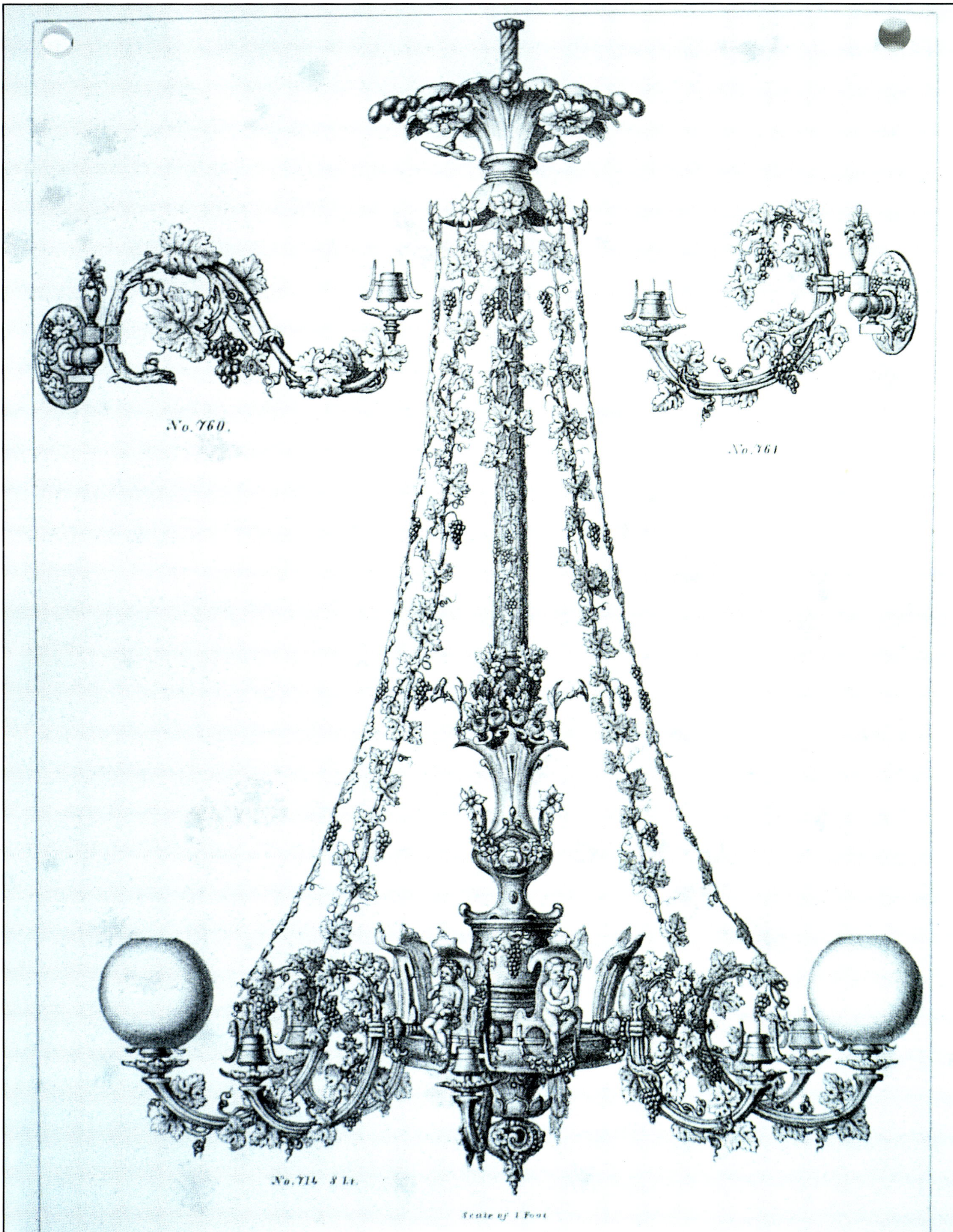

Clockwise from left: No. 760: gas bracket; No. 761: gas wall bracket; No. 714: gas chandelier.

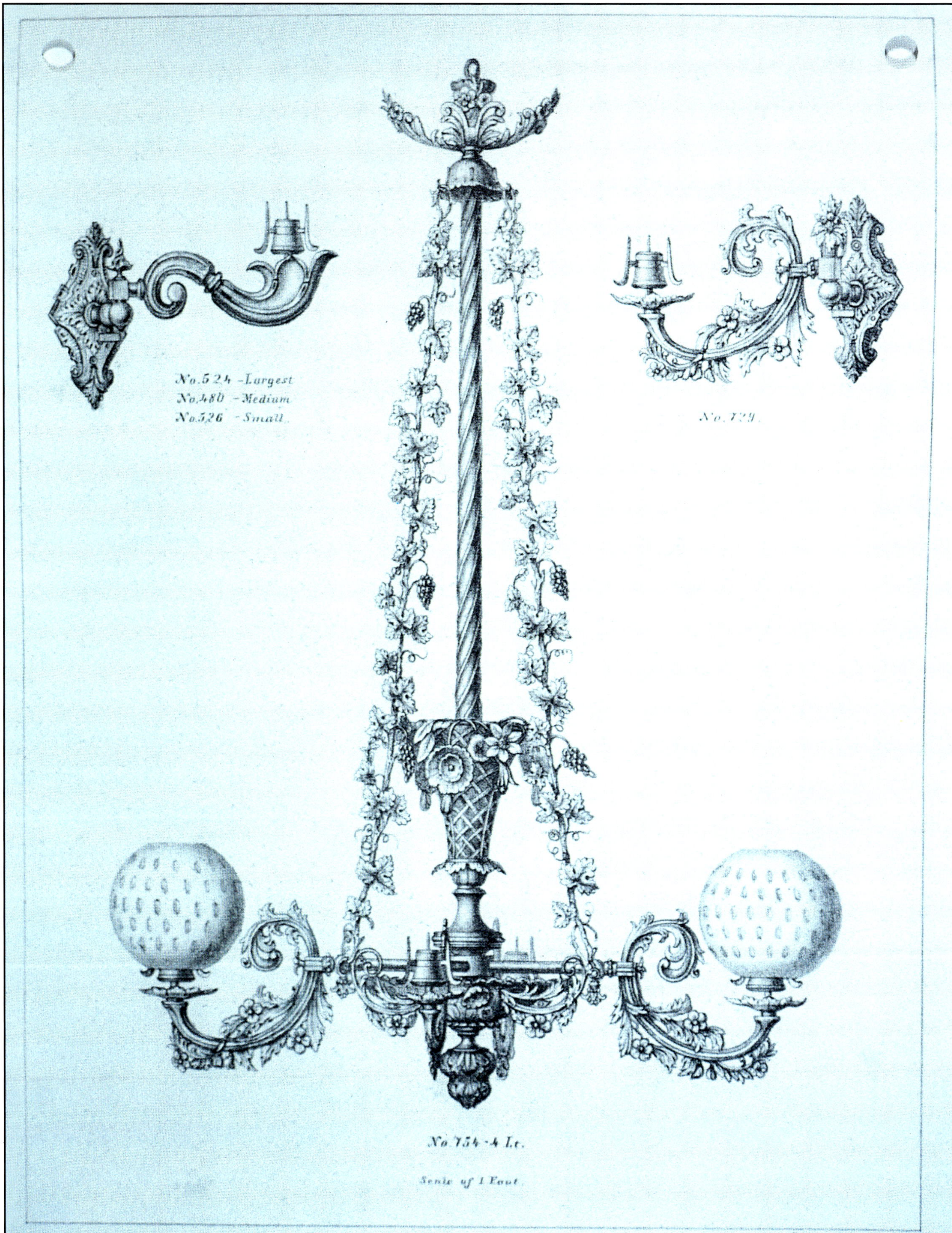

Clockwise from left: Nos. 524, 480, 526: gas bracket;
No. 729: gas wall bracket; No. 754: gas chandelier.

Clockwise from left: No. 659: girandole; No. 420: girandole; No. 706: hanging candelabra.

Clockwise from left: No. 557: gas bracket; No. 759: gas bracket; Nos. 692, 693, 694: gas chandelier.

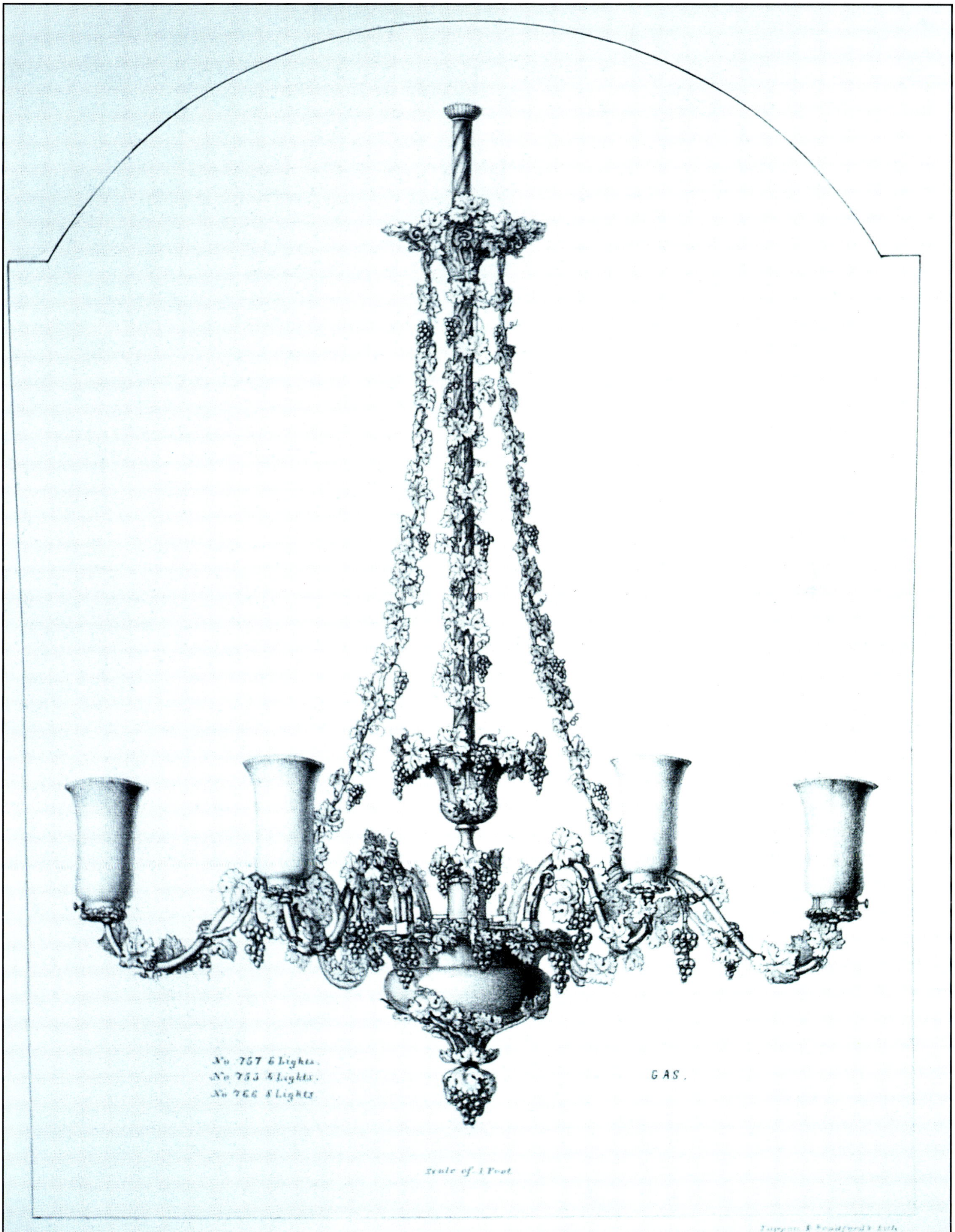

Nos. 757, 755, 766: gas chandelier.

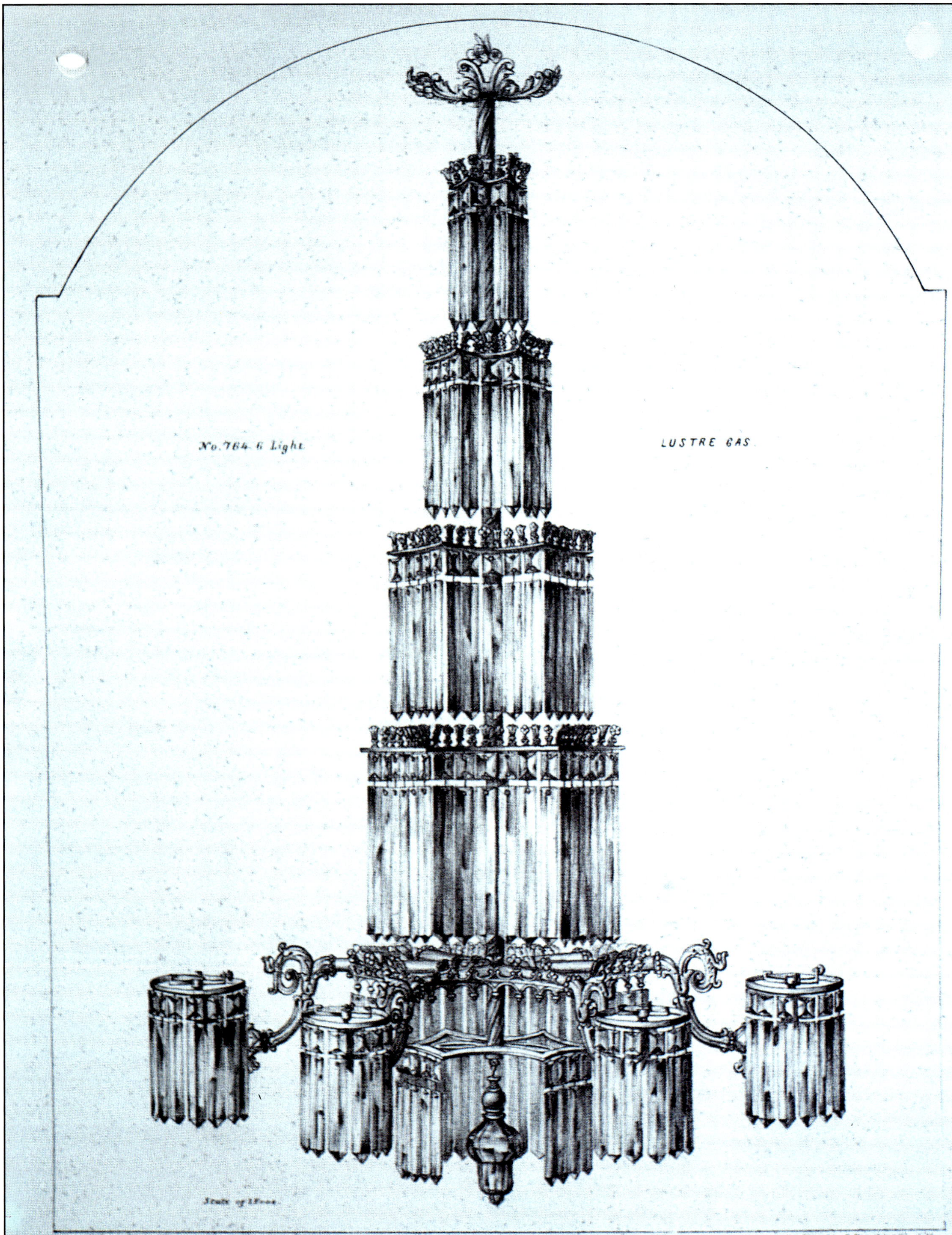

No. 764: gas chandelier.

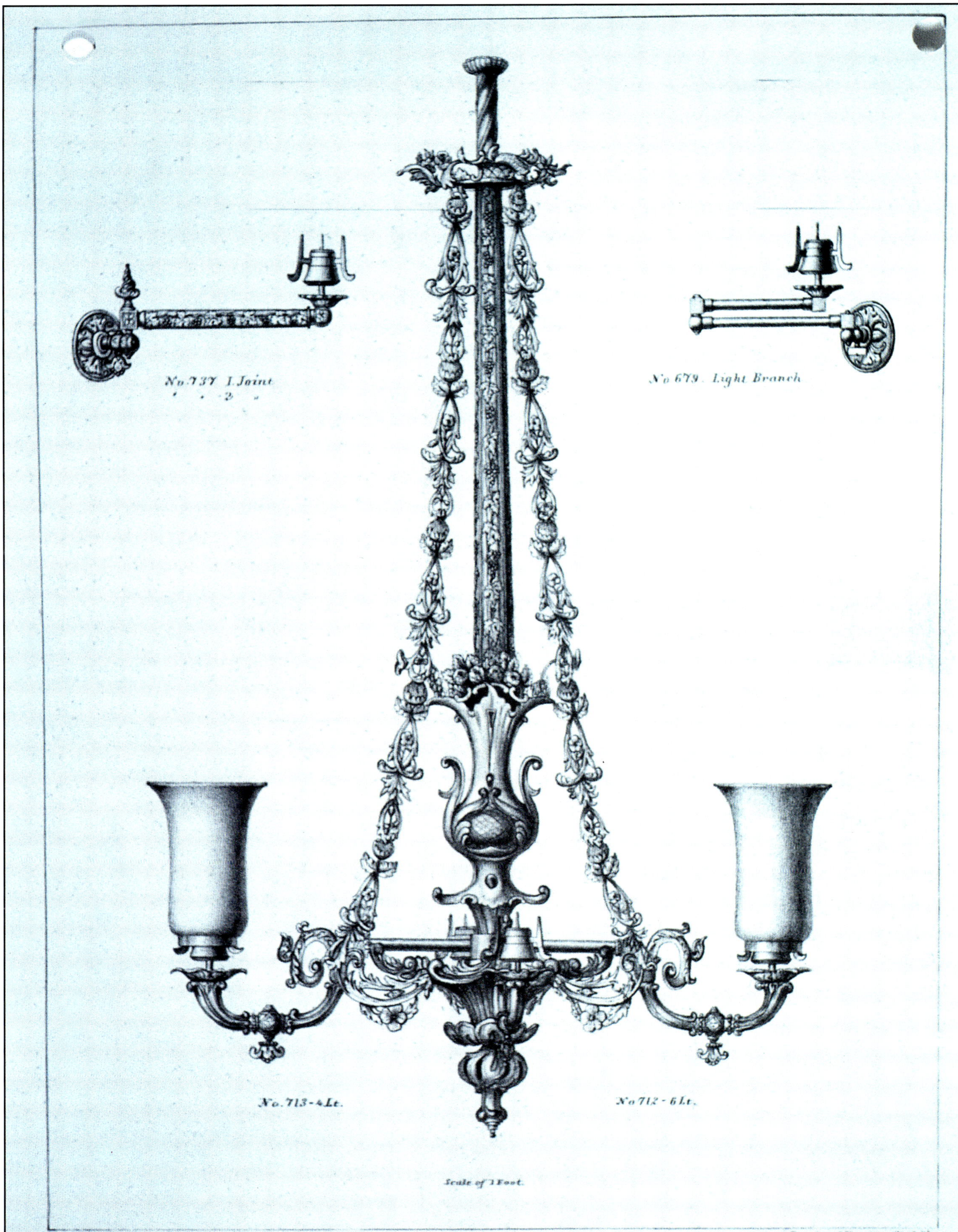

Clockwise from left: No. 737: gas bracket; No. 679: gas bracket; Nos. 712, 713: gas chandelier.

Nos. 756, 775: gas chandelier.

Left to right: No. 738: gas pendant; No. 686: gas pendant; No. 680: gas pendant.

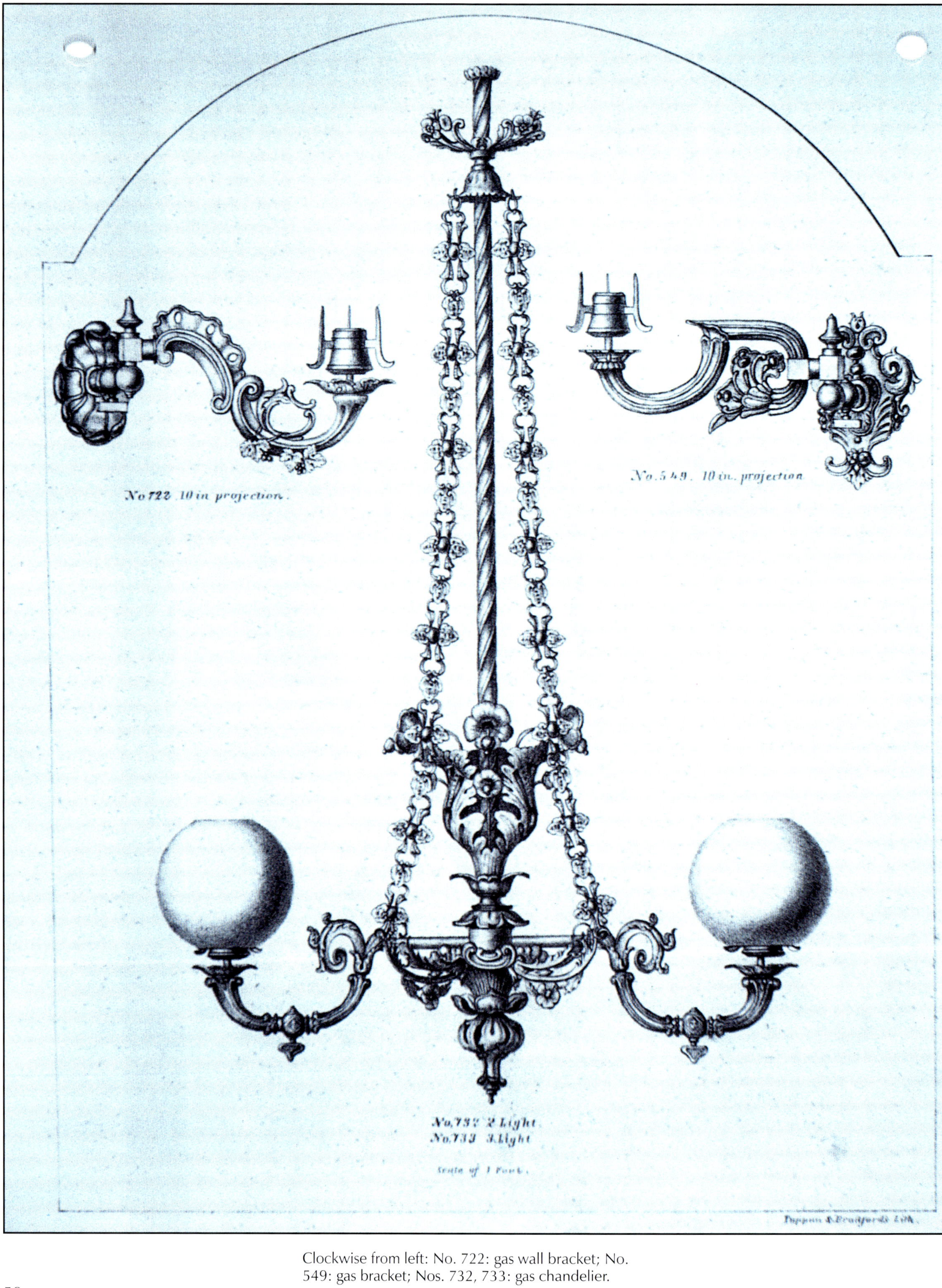

Clockwise from left: No. 722: gas wall bracket; No. 549: gas bracket; Nos. 732, 733: gas chandelier.

Nos. 642, 669: gas chandelier.

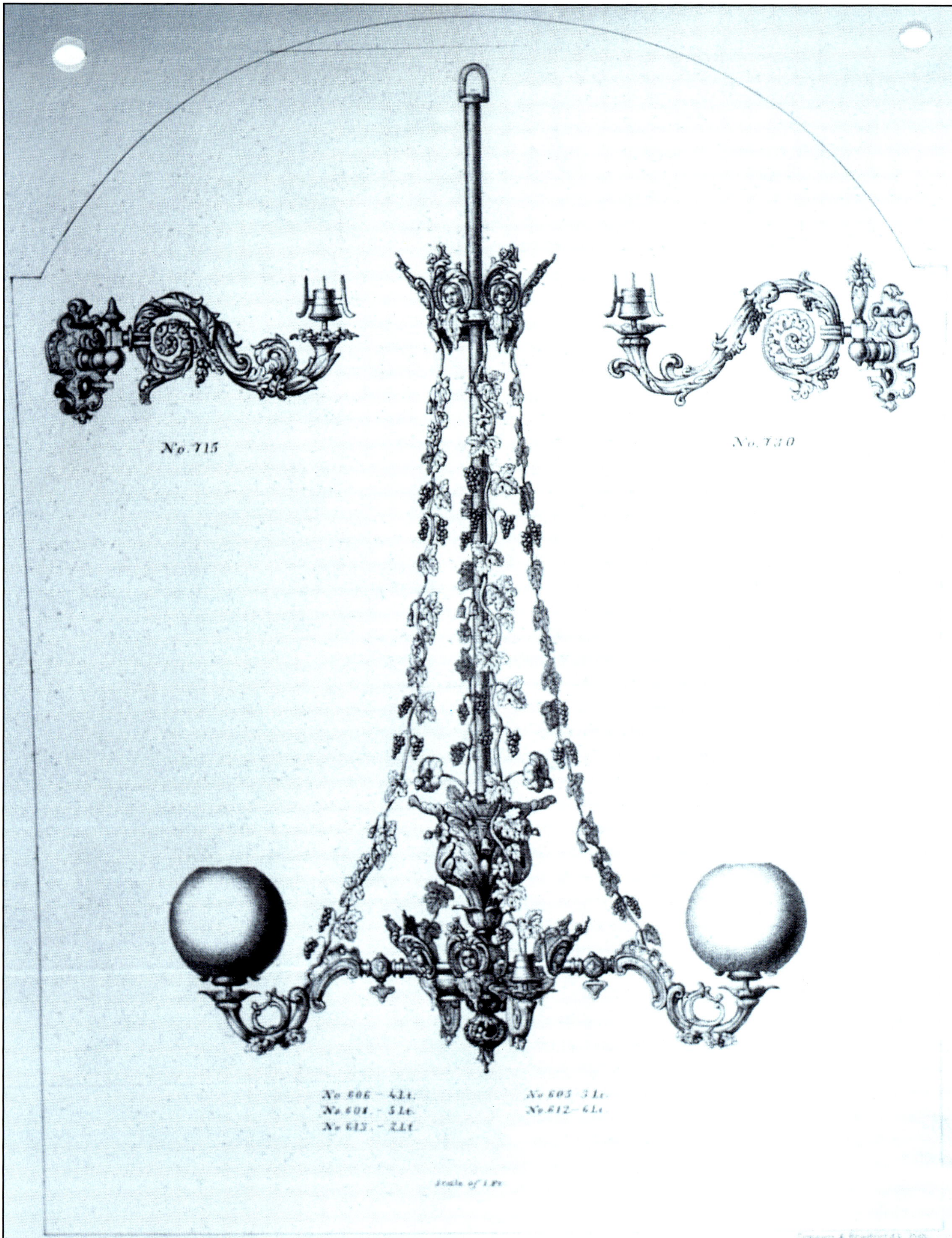

Clockwise from left: No. 715: gas bracket; No. 730: gas branch; Nos. 606, 608, 613, 605, 612: gas chandelier.

Top row, left to right: medium state room lamp (no number assigned); No. 575: solar stand lamp; No. 624: solar stand lamp; Bottom row, left to right: No. 495: girandole; No. 352: girandole.

Top row, left to right: No. 266: girandole; No. 666: girandole; Bottom row, left to right: grapevine boquet (sic, no number assigned); Nos. 740, 596: girandole or mirror painting; No. 455: solar stand lamp.

Left to right: No. 346: solar stand lamp; No. 611: solar stand lamp; No. 176: figural stand lamp (not listed in the Descriptive Catalogue); No. 758: solar stand lamp.

Top row, left to right: No. 505: solar stand lamp; No. 413: girandole; No. 402: solar stand lamp; Bottom row, left to right: No. 656: girandole; No. 462: girandole.

Clockwise from left: No. 781: gas bracket; No. 782 gas bracket; No. 576 (No. does not match with Descriptive Catalogue): gas chandelier.

No. 511: gas chandelier.

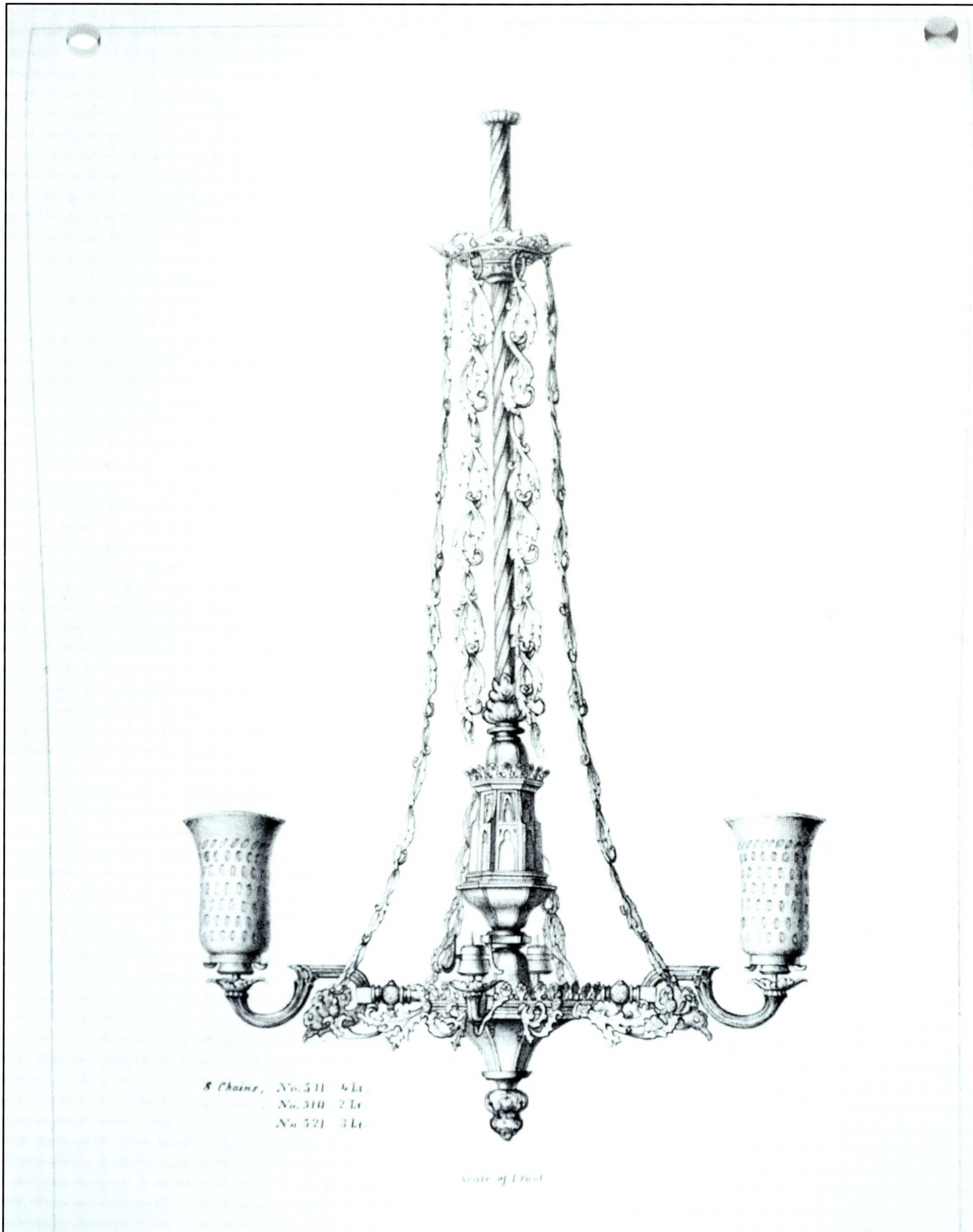

Nos. 511, 510, 521: gas chandelier.

Clockwise from left: No. 529: gas bracket; No. 527: gas bracket; No. 723: gas chandelier.

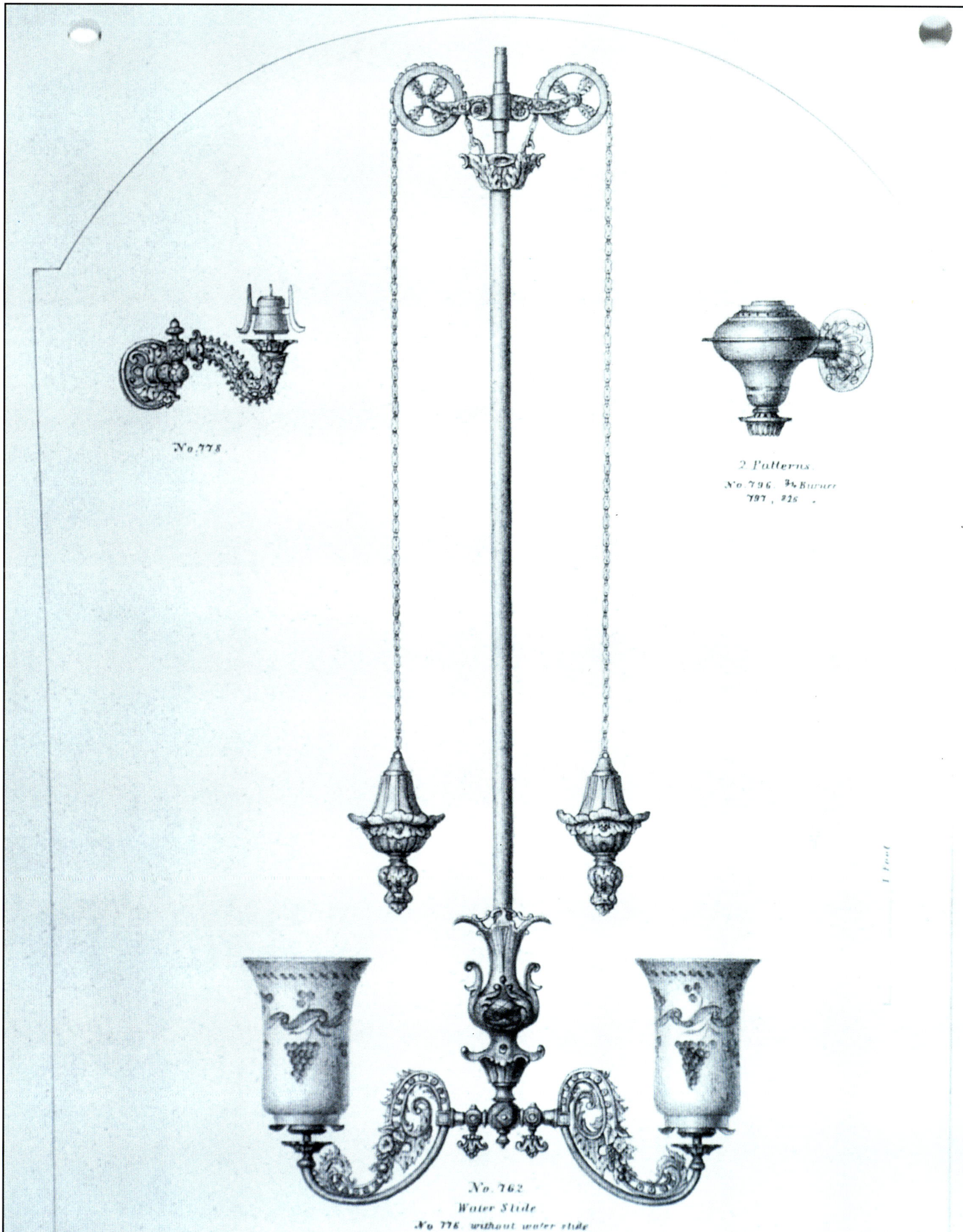

Clockwise from left: No. 778: gas bracket; Nos. 796, 797: solar wall bracket (not listed in the Descriptive Catalogue); No. 762: gas chandelier.

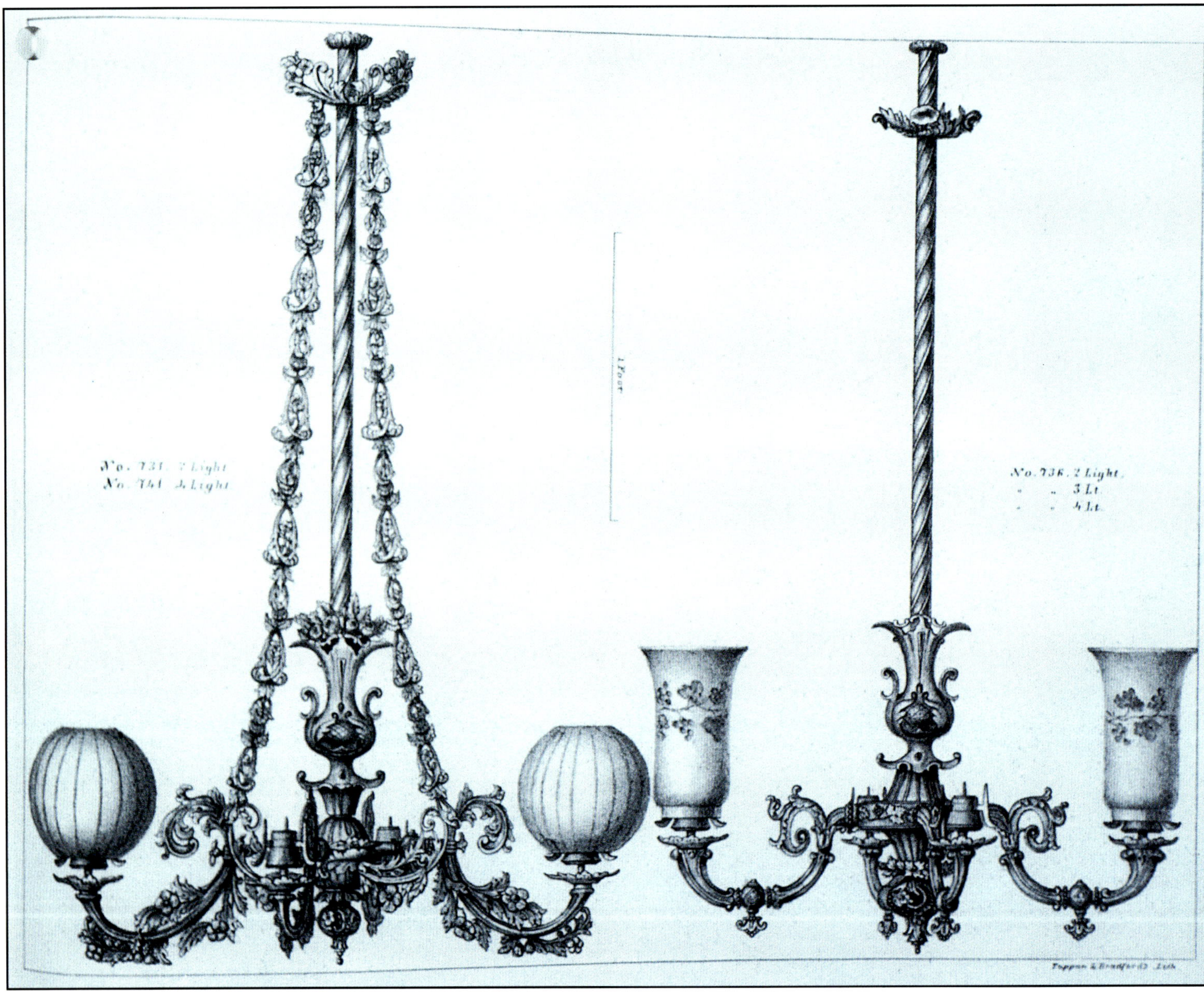

Left to right: Nos. 731, 741: gas chandelier; No. 736: gas pendant.

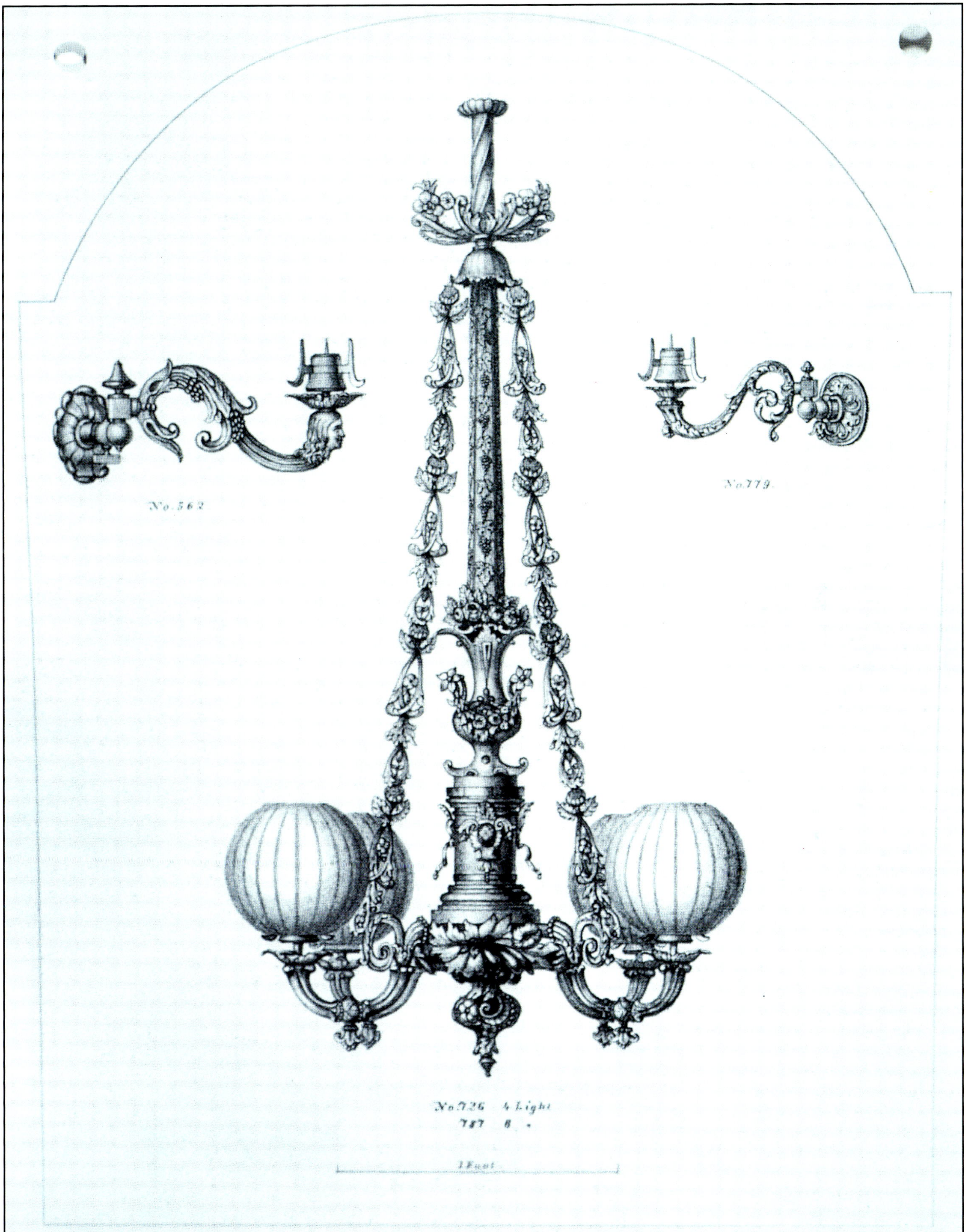

Clockwise from left: No. 562: gas bracket; No. 779: gas bracket; Nos. 726, 787: gas chandelier.

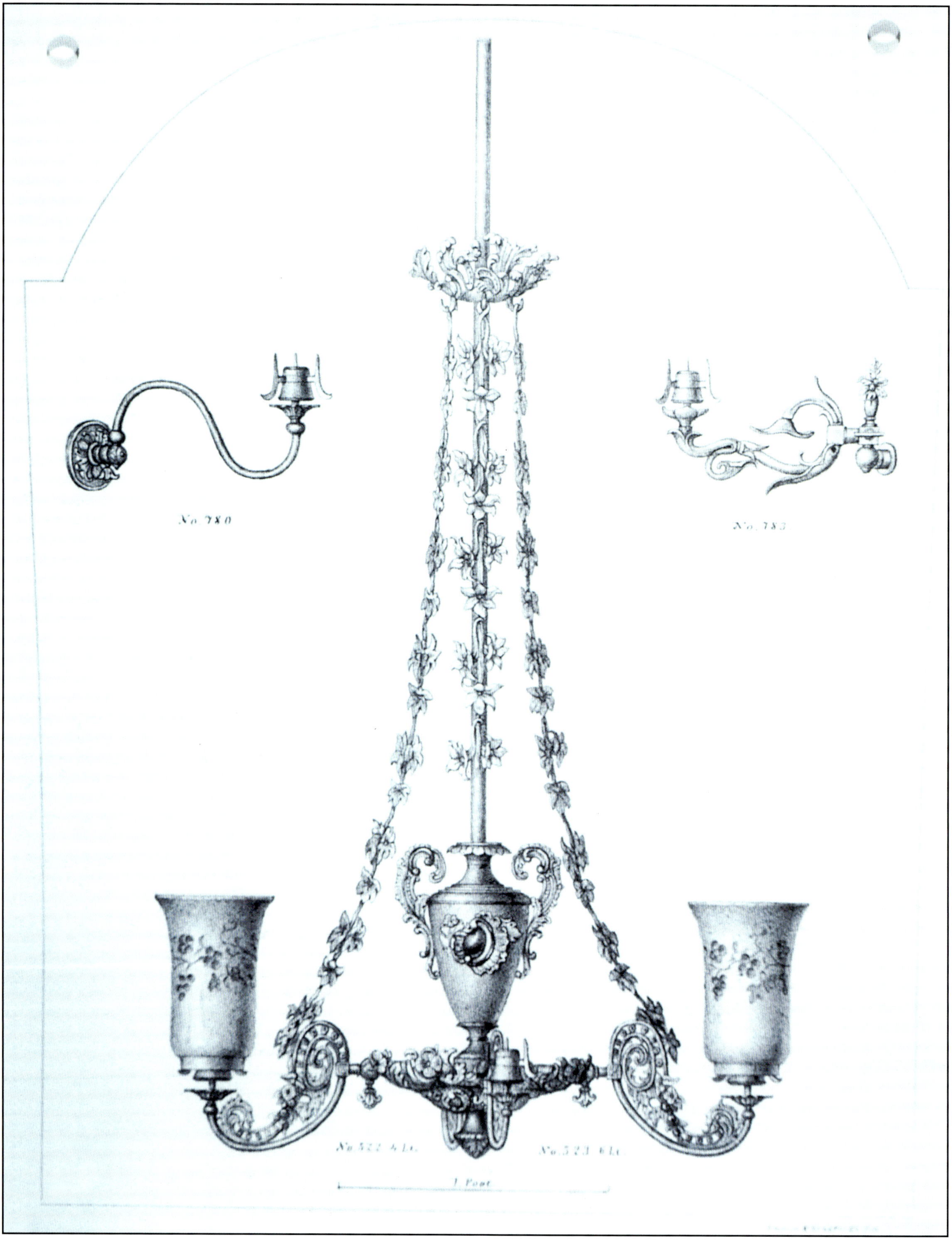

Clockwise from left: No. 780: gas bracket; No. 783: gas bracket; Nos. 522, 523: gas chandelier.

Clockwise from left: No. 728: gas wall bracket; No. 728: gas wall bracket; No. 753: gas girandole; No. 743: girandole.

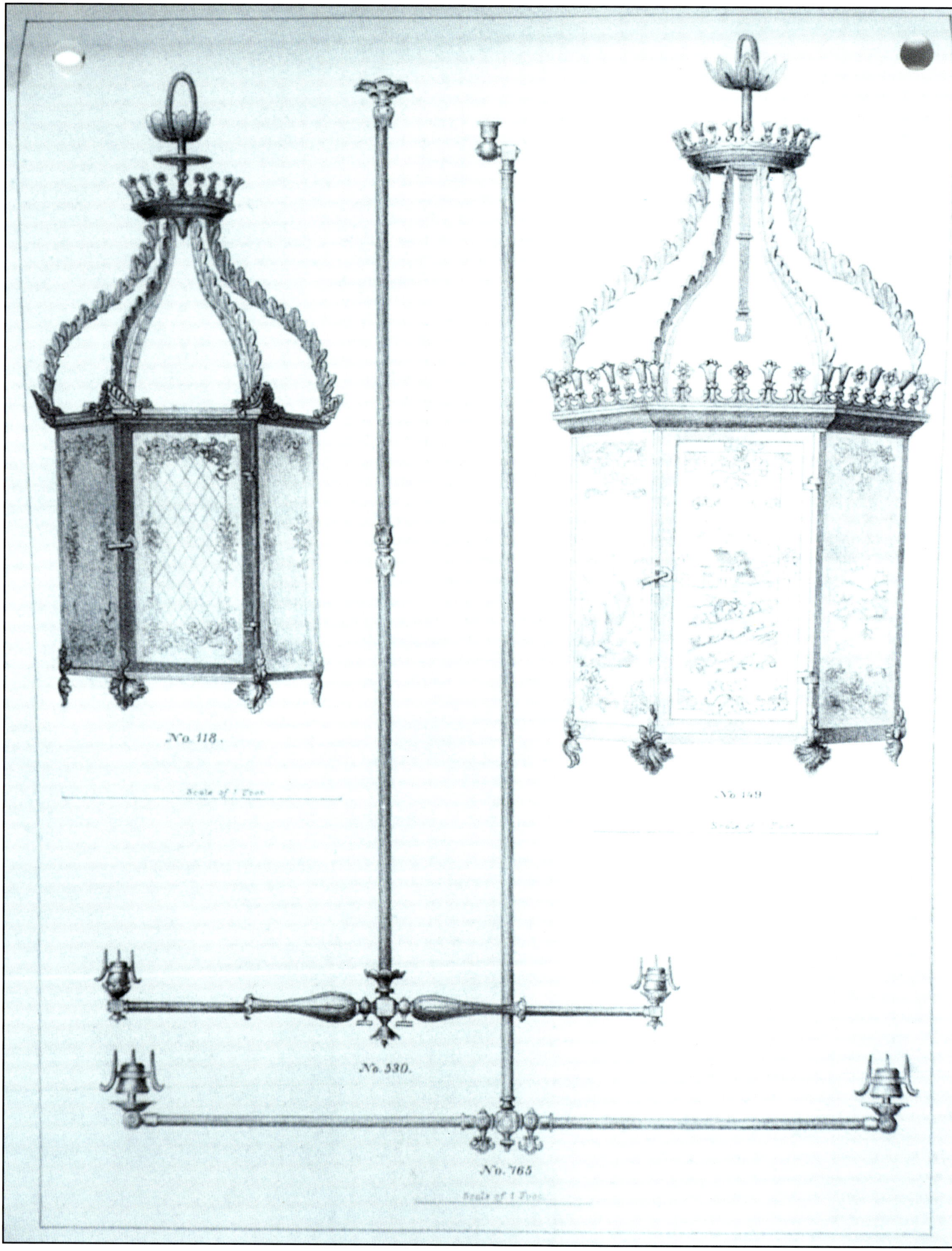

Clockwise from left: No. 118: hall lantern; No. 149: hall lantern; No. 765: gas pendant; No. 530: gas store pendant.

Clockwise from left: No. 461: girandole; girandole (no number assigned); No. 398: Jackson's chemical lamp; No. 700: girandole; No. 520: entry lantern.

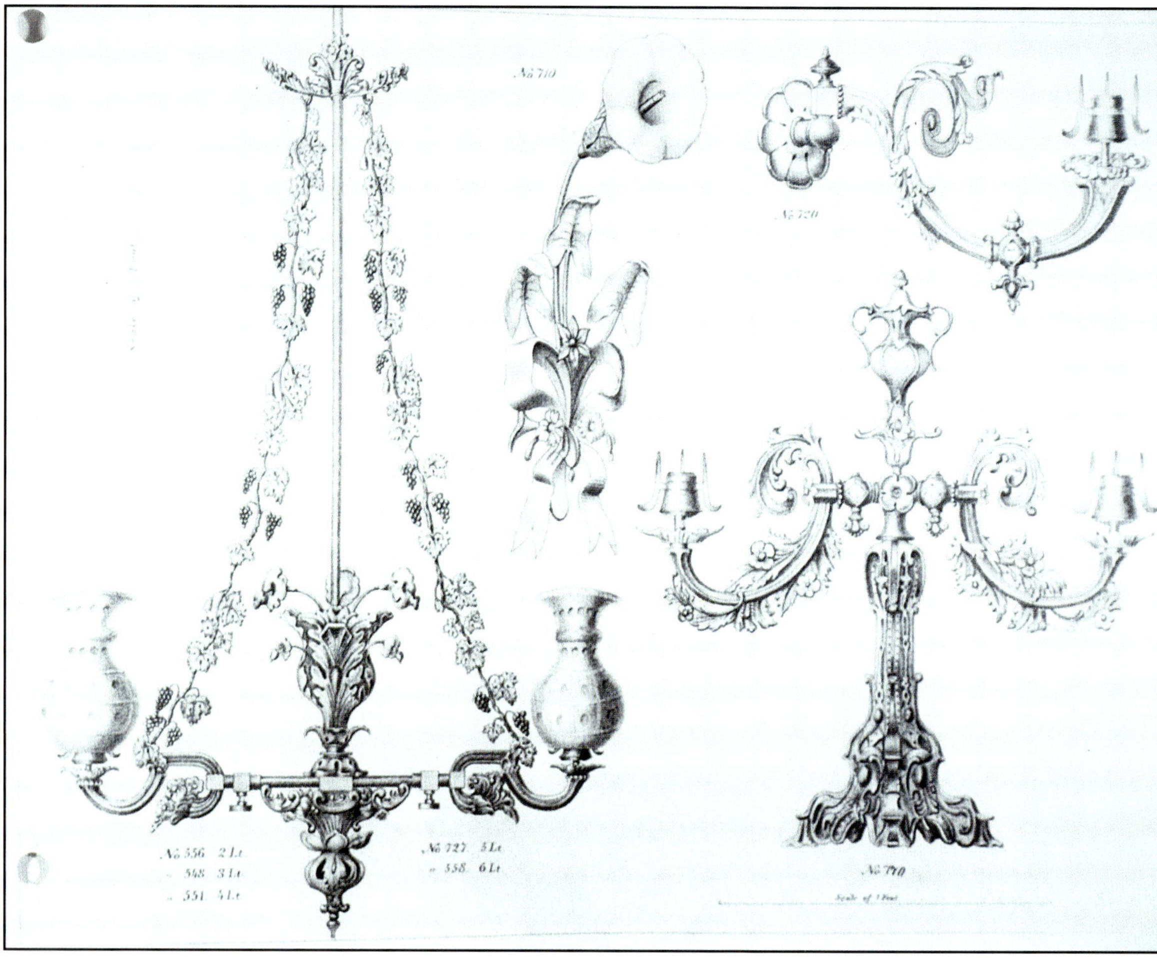

Top row, left to right: No. 710: gas wall bracket; No. 720: gas wall bracket; Bottom row, left to right: Nos. 556, 548, 551, 727, 558: gas chandelier; No. 770: gas girandole.

Back cover of the original 1850 Hooper catalogue.

Patinated bronze two light Argand lamp attributed to Henry N. Hooper and Company, Boston, second quarter nineteenth century, and illustrated as item No. 176 in their 1850 catalogue. This particular item number is not listed in the descriptive contents section of the catalogue. The cut and etched blown glass shades are decorated with berries and vines. The standard is in the form of Nike, the Greek goddess of Victory. Hoisted above her head is a basket of fruit that supports the branches of an urn shaped font. Clusters of fruit decorate the pedestal that rests on a concave plinth. In original condition. Overall height: 36.5". $20,000-$30,000.

Labeled Henry N. Hooper and Company gilt lacquered brass and bronze Jackson Chemical Lamp, second quarter nineteenth century, and illustrated as item No. 398 in their 1850 catalogue. This lamp contains an Argand burner and its design suggests the later developed student lamp. The tole shade is original. The burner plate is inscribed: "H. N. Hooper & Co Boston." The surface is restored. Overall height: 24". $2,000-$3,000.

Gilt lacquered and patinated brass and bronze sinumbra lamp attributed to Henry N. Hooper and Company, Boston, second quarter nineteenth century, and depicted in their 1850 catalogue as item No. 77. These lamps were available in two sizes: No. 1-14.5" or No. 2-16.5". Measurements indicate the height between the top of the drip cup and the bottom of the plinth. The font supports a cut and etched blown glass shade with a base diameter of 8". The tapered standard is raised on a pedestal resting on a square plinth. In original condition. Height to the shade ring: 16.5". Overall height: 23.75". $7,5000-$10,000.

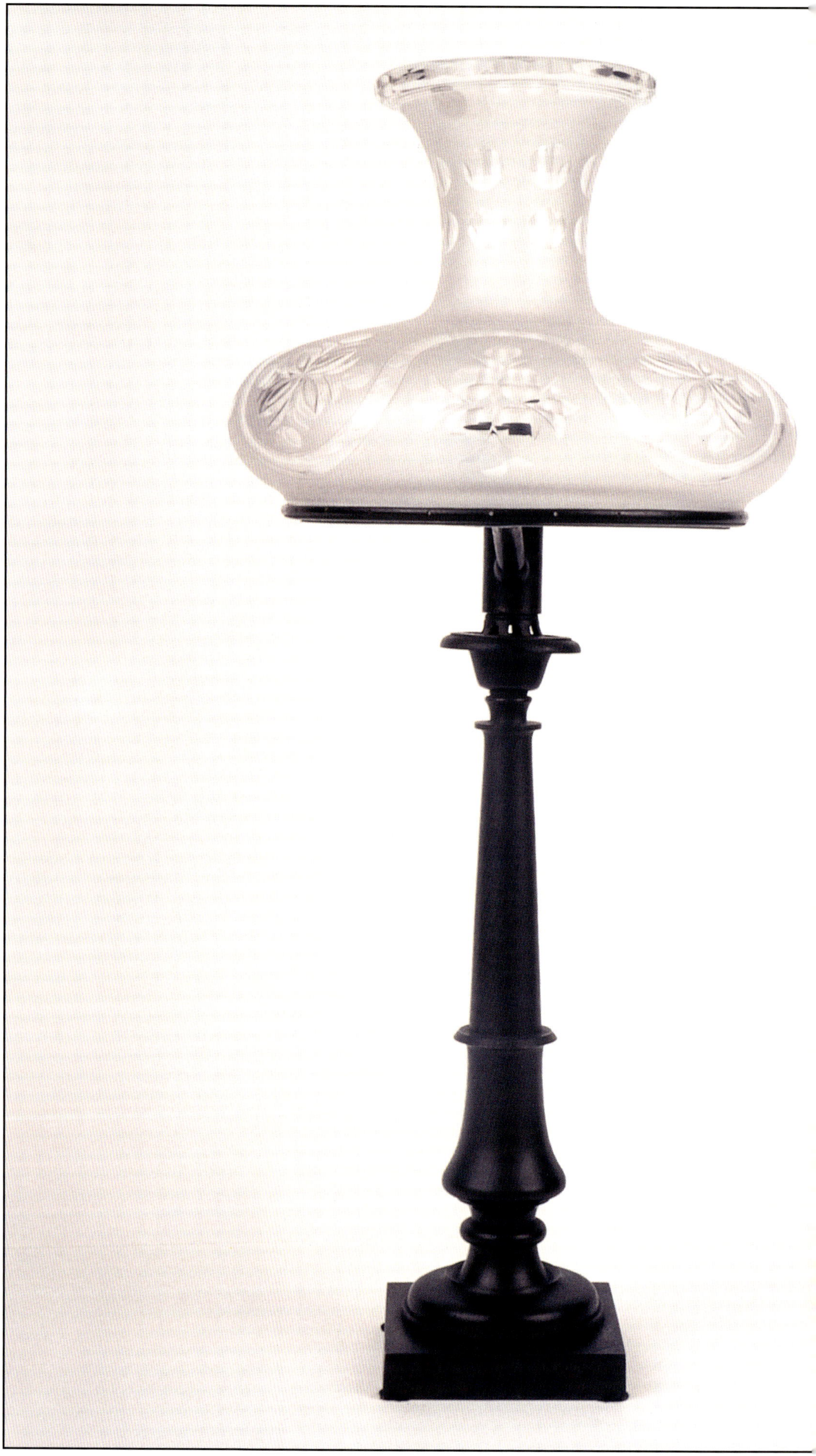

Labeled Henry N. Hooper and Company patinated bronze sinumbra lamp, second quarter nineteenth century, identified as item No. 152 in their 1850 catalogue. It was available in four sizes, although the only one listed in the catalogue is 14.5". The cut and etched blown glass shade is ornamented with flowers and vines. The bulbous standard rests on a square plinth. In original condition. Height to the shade ring: 14.5". Overall height: 21". $7,000-$9,000.

One of a pair of signed, gilt lacquered brass hanging sinumbra lamps, second quarter nineteenth century. The label affixed to the burner tube is inscribed: "Manufactured by H. N. Hooper & Co. Boston." This item probably predates the 1850 Hooper catalogue, as it is not pictured in that document. The cut and etched blown glass globe has a 9" fitter diameter and is decorated with geometric and floral designs. Suspension chains connect the corona and original smoke bell to the support brackets that are in the form of leaves and berries. The surface is restored. Overall length: 25.25". $20,000-$25,000 for the pair.

Labeled gilt lacquered brass hanging sinumbra lamp illustrated in the 1850 Hooper catalogue as item No. 630 (with solar burner), second quarter nineteenth century. The burner label is embossed: "Manufactured by H. N. Hooper & Co. Boston." The 9" shade ring supports a wonderful blown cut and etched glass shade decorated with musical lyres. The shade's neck and rim are faceted. Three foliated branches emerge from the font and are connected to the original glass smoke bell by suspension chains. The surface is restored. Overall height: 20.75". $9,000-$12,000.

Gilt lacquered brass and lacquered brass three light camphene burning chandelier attributed to Henry N. Hooper and Company, second quarter nineteenth century, and depicted in their 1850 catalogue as item No. 361. Each font is fitted with a six-spout camphene burner. The cut and etched blown glass globes have unusual 6.5" fitter diameters. Extending from the central dish are three foliated brackets that support each font. Colonial pendants hang from the fonts and central dish. An additional pendant ring is located on the mid-central support shaft. Extending between the corona and the foliated brackets are chains composed of coupled leaves. The surface is restored. Overall height: 28.75". $15,000-$18,000.

Labeled Hooper and Company gilt lacquered brass and bronze solar lamp, c. 1850, identified as item No. 501 in their 1850 catalogue. Interestingly, the standard is also illustrated in the Dietz catalogue on Plate 32, item No. 47. The double waisted cut and etched blown glass shade has a 6" fitter and rests on a font containing a 3/4" burner stamped: "H N Hooper Boston." In original condition. Height to the shade ring: 18.75". Overall height: 29". $4,000-$5,000.

Opposite page;

Left: Gilt lacquered brass and bronze solar lamp attributed to Henry N. Hooper and Company, c. 1850, and depicted as item No. 356 in their 1850 catalogue. The cut and etched blown glass shade has a 6" wide fitter that rests upon a font containing a 3/4" burner. The Ionic columnar standard is raised on a stepped plinth. The surface is restored. Height to the shade ring: 21". Overall height: 30". $4,000-$5,000.

Right: Gilt lacquered brass and bronze solar lamp attributed to Henry N. Hooper and Company, c. 1850, and depicted in their 1850 catalogue as item No. 432. The bulbous "Oregon" style cut and etched blown glass top mount shade has a 2.5" wide fitter that rests on a 9/16" burner. The standard is raised on a square marble plinth. In original condition. Height to the top of the font: 12". Overall height: 20.5". $800-$1,200.

Gilt lacquered brass and bronze solar lamp attributed to Henry N. Hooper and Company, c. 1850, and identified in their 1850 catalogue as item No. 636. A version of this model also appears in the Starr, Fellows catalogue of 1856 as item No. 250 (with button feet). The bulbous cut and etched blown glass globe with a rolled rim and a 6" fitter diameter rests on a font containing a 3/4" burner. The standard is ornamented by cabochons and terminates in scroll feet. In original condition. Height to the shade ring: 13.75". Overall height: 24.5". $2,000-$2,500.

Gilt lacquered brass and bronze solar lamp attributed to Henry N. Hooper and Company, c. 1850, relating to item No. 591 in their 1850 catalogue. The spherical form ribbed and etched blown glass shade has a 5" wide fitter and rests on an urn shaped font containing a 9/16" burner. At one time, crystal pendants were suspended from the delicate leaves that lie atop the standard. The columnar standard is raised on a square white marble plinth. The surface is restored. Height to the shade ring: 12.5". Overall height: 19.75". $1,500-$2,000.

Gilt lacquered brass and polished brass solar lamp attributed to Henry N. Hooper and Company, c. 1850, and illustrated in their 1850 catalogue as item No. 336. Classical lyres and gothic windows ornament the ball form cut and etched blown glass shade with a 6" wide fitter. The font contains a 3/4" burner. The vintage pattern tier supports snowflake pendants. The fluted pedestal rests upon a square plinth. The surface is restored. Height to the shade ring: 12.375". Overall height: 20.75". $2,000-$2,500.

Signed rare gilt lacquered brass and bronze adjustable solar student lamp, c.1850, not found in the 1850 Hooper catalogue. The 9/16" burner is stamped: "H. N. Hooper Boston." The standard has a ring finial and is raised above a spreading socle. The adjustable branch supports the inverted pear shaped font and an "Oregon" style, top mount cut and etched blown glass shade with a 2.5" fitter. The surface is restored. Height to the top of the standard: 17.5". $1,800-$2,200.

Spectacular signed pair of gilt lacquered brass and bronze solar lamps, c.1850. These lamps are not found in the Hooper catalogue. Both fonts are fitted with 3/4" burners, each supporting ball form finely cut and etched blown glass shades with 6" fitters. Stamped on the burners is: "Hooper & Co Boston Solar." In addition, the second brass casting from the bottom is inscribed: "Published As The Act Directs Messenger & Sons Birmingham." There are many reasonable scenarios as to how Hooper burners are found on Messenger castings. However, it is highly unlikely that anyone knows the correct answer. Arguably, these lamps have been left in the Hooper section of the book. However, the author would not take issue with anyone wishing to reassign these lamps to the Messenger chapter. Albert pendants are suspended from the grape clustered calices serving as the drip cups. The two entwined dancing muses comprise the standard that surmounts a cylindrical pedestal decorated with applied ormolu arabesque festoons. This base rests on an octagonal plinth. The surface is restored. Height to the shade ring: 25". Overall height: 33". $18,000-$22,000 for the pair.

Signed Hooper gilt lacquered brass and bronze solar lamp, c. 1850, not illustrated in their 1850 catalogue. The ball form cut and etched blown glass globe has a 5" wide fitter that rests on a font containing a 3/4" burner, which is stamped: "Hooper & Co Boston Solar." The fluted standard is raised on a square marble plinth. In original condition. Height to the shade ring: 13". Overall height: 23". $600-$1,000.

Gilt lacquered brass and bronze solar lamp attributed to Henry N. Hooper and Company, c. 1850, and depicted in their 1850 catalogue as item No. 601. The spherical form blown and etched glass shade with a 6" diameter fitter rests on a font containing a 3/4" burner. The standard is foliated and designed with cartouches and cabochons. The triangular plinth terminates in scroll feet. In original condition. Height to the shade ring: 20". Overall height: 29". $4,000-$5,000.

Gilt lacquered brass and bronze solar lamp attributed to Henry N. Hooper and Company, Boston, c. 1850, and illustrated as item No. 619 in their 1850 catalogue. The cut and etched blown glass shade has a faceted everted neck, rolled rim, and a 5" wide fitter. The font retains its original burner elements. The standard, which rests on a double marble plinth, is embossed with a likeness of Martha Washington. In original condition. Height to the top of the shade ring: 13". Overall height: 23". $3,000-$4,000.

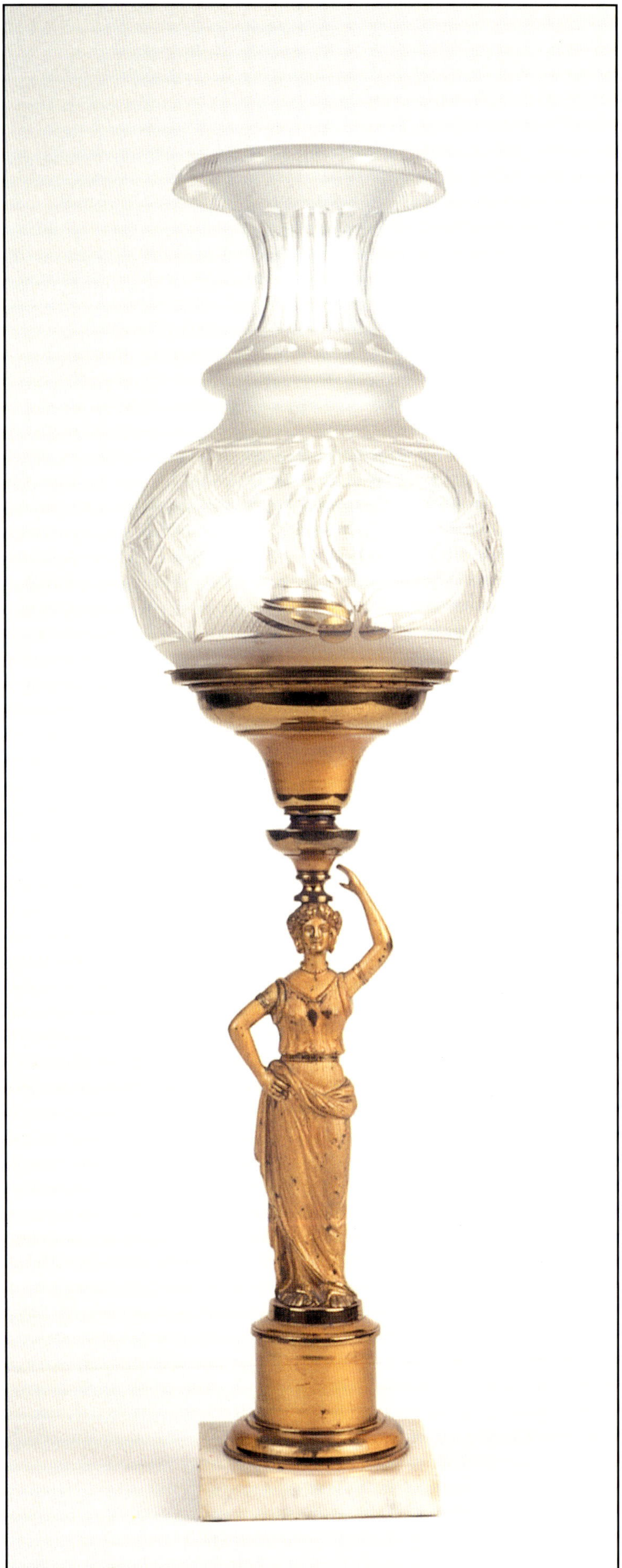

Gilt lacquered brass and bronze solar lamp, c. 1850, identified as item No. 505 in the 1850 Hooper catalogue and also on Plate 32, item No. 149 in the 1860 Dietz catalogue. The lamp has also been found bearing the label of Cornelius and Sons, Philadelphia. This is yet another example of the integration of metal castings among lighting manufacturers. The double waisted cut and etched blown glass globe rests on a font containing its original burner components. The standard is in the form of a classical maiden wearing a chiton while holding one hand on her head, the other resting on her hip. She is raised on a circular pedestal resting on a square marble plinth. In original condition. Height to the shade ring: 18". Overall height: 31". $5,000-$6,000.

Gilt brass and lacquered brass and bronze solar lamp attributed to Henry N. Hooper and Company, c. 1850, and identified as item No. 620 in their 1850 catalogue. The ball form cut and etched blown glass globe with a 5" wide fitter rests on a font containing a 9/16" burner. A separate ring below the shade ring supports 3" long faceted crystal pendants. The fluted standard rests on a double marble plinth bordered by gilt bronze leaves. In original condition. Height to the shade ring: 11". Overall height: 18". $1,000-$1,500.

Gilt lacquered brass and bronze solar lamp attributed to Henry N. Hooper and Company, c. 1850, and shown in their 1850 catalogue as item No. 402. The ball form ribbed, etched and blown glass globe has a fitter width of 6" and rests on a font containing a 3/4" burner. The columnar standard is raised on a double marble plinth. The surface is restored. Height to the shade ring: 16.75". Overall height: 24.5". $1,800-$2,200.

Gilt lacquered and patinated brass and bronze solar lamp attributed to Henry N. Hooper and Company, c. 1850, and identified as item No. 467 in their 1850 catalogue. The font containing a 3/4" burner supports a spherical form cut and etched blown glass shade decorated with gothic windows. The breather appears to be modeled as a candle cup. The standard is raised on a pedestal resting on a square plinth. In original condition. Height to the shade ring: 14.75". Overall height: 22.25". $1,800-$2,200.

Gilt bronze six light candelabra (left) attributed to Henry N. Hooper and Company of Boston, c. 1850, and identified in their 1850 catalogue as item No. 579. The solar lamp (right) relates to the Hooper catalogue item No. 502. Although the plinths of these two items are different, the standards are identical. Lamp manufacturers of the time showed versatility by incorporating interchangeable castings to create new designs and different products. Candelabra: $1,200-$1,500. Solar lamp: $2,500-$3,000.

Detail of previous candelabra branch illustrating how various casting elements may be combined to create a new design. In this case, the standard was actually made as a baluster with a breather for a solar lamp. The plate to which the branches are attached is treaded and screws into the top of the standard the same as a solar font.

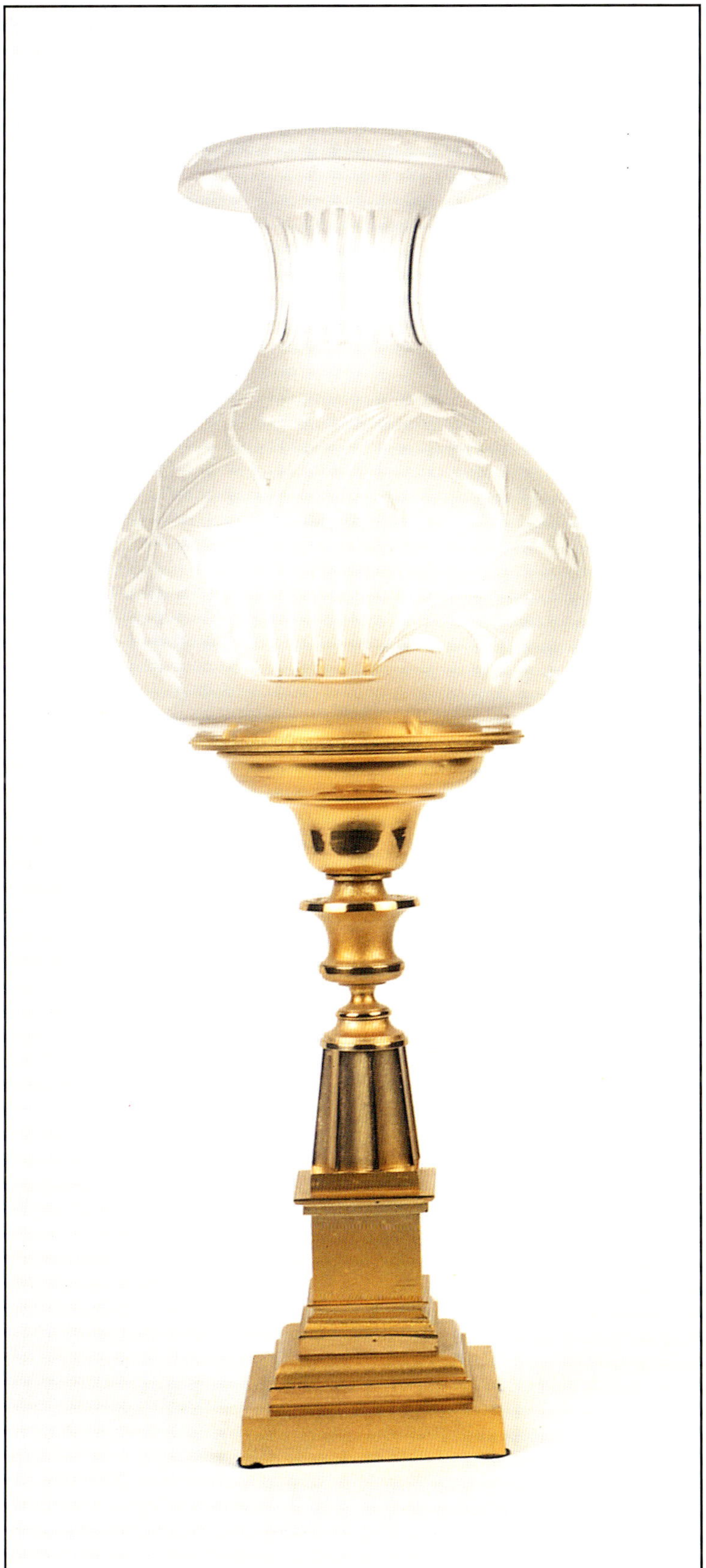

Signed Hooper gilt lacquered brass and bronze solar lamp, c. 1850, relating to item No. 456 in their 1850 catalogue. The floral cut and etched blown glass shade has a 5" wide fitter and rests on a font containing a 3/4" burner. The fluted standard is raised on a rectangular pedestal and stepped plinth. The cast iron base weight contained within the plinth is stamped: "H N Hooper and Co No 4." In original condition. Height to the shade ring: 10". Overall height: 19.75". $1,800-$2,200.

Gilt and lacquered brass and bronze solar lamp attributed to Henry N. Hooper and Company, c. 1850, and shown in their 1850 catalogue as item No. 627. The intricately cut and etched blown glass shade has a 5" fitter, an inverted neck, a rolled rim, and rests on an urn form font containing a 9/16" burner. The design of the standard is sometimes referred to as an "Iris" pattern (see pages 34, 35, and 203). The standard also appears in the 1860 Dietz catalogue, on Plate 32, item No. 154. The standard rests on a white double marble plinth. The surface is restored. Height to the shade ring: 13". Overall height: 24". $3,000-$4,000.

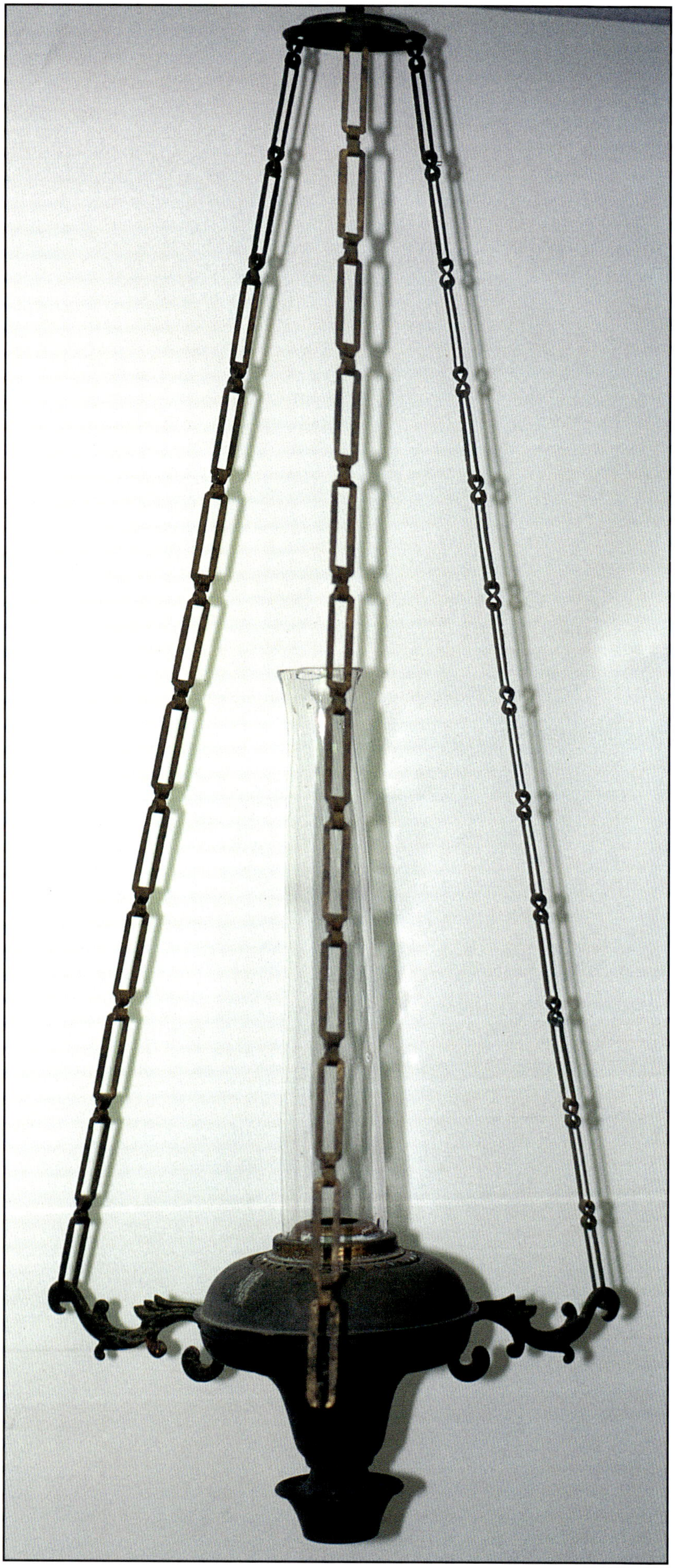

Hanging brass solar lamp attributed to Henry N. Hooper and Company, c.1850, and depicted in their 1850 catalogue as item No. 498. Similar lamps are found in the oil hanging section of the 1856 Starr, Fellows catalogue and in the 1860 Dietz catalogue on Plate 31, item No. 19. A circular bracket holds the font, which retains its original burner components. A glass chimney rests on the burner. Alternating rectangular and circular links of chain connect the three foliated brackets to the disc shaped corona. In original condition. Overall length: 54.5". $3,000-$4,000.

Labeled Hooper gilt lacquered brass and bronze solar lamp, c. 1850, identified as item No. 419 in their 1850 catalogue. The 3/4" burner is stamped: "Hooper & Co Boston Solar." The font supports a ball form cut and etched blown glass shade having a 5" diameter fitter. The figural standard probably depicts Romeo standing on a foliated pedestal and square marble plinth. In original condition. Height to the shade ring: 12.5". Overall height: 19.25". $2,500-$3,000.

Detail of the burner deflector as seen in previous solar lamp.

Gilt lacquered brass and bronze solar lamp attributed to Henry N. Hooper and Company, c. 1850, and identified as item No. 699 in their 1850 catalogue. Note that a set screw holds the cut and etched blown glass shade firmly at the base. The bulbous standard is raised on a square white marble plinth. In original condition. Height to the top of the font: 12". Overall height: 20". $1,800-$2,200.

Gilt lacquered brass and polished brass solar lamp attributed to Henry N. Hooper and Company, c. 1850, and illustrated as item No. 631 in their 1850 catalogue. The cut and etched blown glass shade with an everted rim, faceted neck, and a 5" diameter fitter is decorated with gothic windows. The font is fitted with a 9/16" burner. The columnar standard is raised on a double white marble plinth. In original condition. Height to the top of the shade ring: 11". Overall height: 20.50". $1,000-$1,500.

Gilt lacquered brass and bronze solar lamp attributed to Henry N. Hooper and Company, c. 1850. This lamp is depicted in the 1850 Hooper catalogue as item No. 396. The bulbous form "Oregon" style floral cut and etched blown glass top mounted shade has a 2.5" wide fitter that rests on a 9/16" burner. The urn form standard is raised on a spreading socle. In original condition. Height to the shade ring: 8". Overall height: 17". $500-$900.

Gilt lacquered brass and bronze solar lamp attributed to Henry N. Hooper and Company, c. 1850, and identified as item No. 590 in their 1850 catalogue. The ball form cut and etched blown glass shade is decorated with cornucopias and has a fitter diameter of 6". The font contains a 3/4" burner. The Ionic columnar standard rests on a spreading foot and square marble plinth. In original condition. Height to the shade ring: 13.75". Overall height: 22". $1,500-$2,500.

Diminutive gilt lacquered brass and bronze whale oil lamp attributed to Henry N. Hooper and Company, c. 1850. A related example is illustrated in the 1850 Hooper catalogue as item No. 995 and is referred to as a medium state room lamp. This lamp is gimbaled. The shade is held in place by a set screw. In original condition. Height to the top of the font: 3.625". Overall height: 6.5". $1,000-$1,500.

Gilt lacquered brass and bronze solar lamp attributed to Henry N. Hooper and Company, c. 1850, and identified as item No. 329 in their 1850 catalogue. The ball form cut and etched blown glass shade has a 6" diameter fitter. The font contains a 3/4" burner. The bulbous standard rests on a square plinth. The surface finish has been restored. Height to the shade ring: 9.25". Overall height: 15.50". $1,800-$2,200.

Pair of gilt lacquered and patinated bronze and brass solar lamps attributed to Henry N. Hooper and Company, c. 1850, and illustrated in their 1850 catalogue as item No. 432 (without the crystal pendants). The fonts contain 3/4" burners. The 5" fitter diameter cut and etched "Oregon" style blown glass globes are decorated with grape clusters and vines. The standards rest on single marble plinths. In original condition. Height to the shade ring: 11.25". Overall height: 21". $2,000-$2,500 for the pair.

A utilitarian gilt brass and tole dual function solar wall sconce and table lamp, c. 1850. This lamp is identified as item No. 400 in the 1850 Hooper catalogue and also as item No. 1 in the 1856 Starr, Fellows catalogue. The font contains a 3/4" burner and supports a tapered chimney and a concave reflector with central convexity. In original condition. Height to the top of the chimney: 16". $500-$600.

Gilt lacquered brass and bronze solar lamp attributed to Henry N. Hooper and Company, c. 1850, and depicted in their 1850 catalogue as item No. 405. The spherical form cut and etched blown glass shade has a 6" diameter fitter and rests on a font containing a 3/4" burner. The Ionic columnar standard is raised on a stepped square plinth. The surface is restored. Height to the shade ring: 15". Overall height: 23.375". $1,800-$2,200.

Pair of English or French gilt and patinated bronze four light candelabras (left). One standard is in the form of a swordsman that is identical to the two Hooper attributed solar lamps to the right. This is an illustration of Hooper's willingness to copy other manufacturer's castings. The gilt lacquered brass and bronze solar lamp (second from right) is identified as item No. 412 in the 1850 Hooper catalogue. The top mount cut and etched blown glass shade has a 2.5" fitter that rests on a 9/16" burner. The swordsman standard is atop a square marble plinth. Height to the top of font: 15". Overall height: 23". $1,800-$2,200. The patinated brass and bronze solar lamp (far right) supports a ball form cut and etched glass shade decorated with geometric motifs. The swordsman standard is raised on a square stepped plinth. Height to the shade ring: 13". Overall height: 26". $2,000-$2,500.

Gilt lacquered brass candlestick attributed to Henry N. Hooper and Company, c. 1850, and illustrated in their 1850 catalogue as item No. 593. Scrolling feet and cabochons comprise the plinth from where the reeded and foliated standard arises. Combined clusters of grapes and their leaves form the ring from which icicle pendants are attached. The surface is restored. Once again this standard is an example of a casting that may be used for either a lamp or candlestick. Overall height: 12.5" $400-$600.

Pair of gilt lacquered brass candelabras attributed to Henry N. Hooper and Company, c. 1850, and found in the 1850 catalogue as item No. 420 (catalogue shows them on a marble base). Pairs of couchant stags rest atop the octagonal plinth. Sinuous branches of curled leaves grow from the reeded standards to support spun brass candle cups with revolute foliage. In original condition. Height: 17". $1,500-$1,800.

A cartouche form watch hutch surmounted by an eagle, together with another watch hutch in the form of a coiled serpent. Both are attributed to Henry N. Hooper and Company and both are illustrated in the 1850 Hooper catalogue but have no item number designations. Scattered throughout the 1850 Hooper catalogue are occasional nonlighting items such as vases and the watch hutches depicted. It is unclear why Hooper advertised these goods in his lighting catalogue. Perhaps they were included to illustrate the diversity of Hooper's products.

Chapter Two

Starr, Fellows and Company

In 1840, William H. Starr and Charles H. Fellows formed a partnership known as Starr, Fellows and Company. For the first several years of its existence, the business exclusively produced lighting devices designed to use burning fluid and later camphene. As best could be determined, the firm never produced Argand or sinumbra lamps. Their manufacturing facility was located in Brooklyn and the warehouse on 74 Beekman Street in Manhattan. Interestingly, Robert Edwin Dietz (see Chapter Three) lived at 66 Beekman Street about the same time.

By the late 1840s, the company—responding to public demand—began to produce gas fixtures and lighting devices using solar burners. In 1846, Starr received a solar lamp patent for a device that more efficiently delivered fuel to the burning portion of the wick.

In their 1856 catalogue, solar lamps are referred to as "oil lamps." Mention is made that ordinary lard and common fish oil burn equally well in their solar lamps.

The entire engraving and some of the drawings in the 1856 catalogue were accomplished by women associated with the New York City School of Design.

In 1857, Starr sold his interest in the company to the remaining partners, consisting of Charles H. Fellows, Charles O. Hoffman, James G. Dolbeare and George Nichols. Jerome G. Comstock was brought in and the business name was changed to Fellows, Hoffman and Company on March 2, 1857. Their location remained on Beekman Street in New York City and they continued in business under one of the two names until 1880.

While the author has seen burning fluid lamps with the company's mark on the burner, typically, Starr, Fellows and Company did not sign their solar lamps. None of the solar lamps illustrated on the following pages bore marks. These lamps were compared to the contents of various makers' catalogues until a particular illustration matched a certain lamp. Because of this lack of markings, please note that all of the lamps in this chapter are "attributed" to Starr, Fellows and Company.

It appears that the 1856 catalogue underwent additions and/or revisions after the departure of William Starr.

Not shown in this text are four pages of their catalogue labeled: "Extra Sheet of New Patterns for 1858 Fellows, Hoffman & Co., 74 Beekman Street." Illustrated on these pages are gasoliers, a solar chandelier, three solar stand lamps, and other miscellaneous gas lights.

In addition, there are four other pages titled: "Fellows, Hoffman & Co., 74 Beekman Street, 1858-1859." These pages contain examples of gas chandeliers and wall sconces, solar stand lamps and chandeliers, and various lighting devices designed to use burning fluid and camphene.

The following pages concerning oil (solar) lamps are taken from the company's 1856 catalogue.

STARR, FELLOWS & CO.'S

ILLUSTRATED CATALOGUE

OF

LAMPS, GAS FIXTURES, &C.

WAREHOUSE, 74 BEEKMAN-ST., NEW YORK.

MANUFACTORY:

NOS. 71, 73, 75, 77, 79, 81, 83 BOERUM-STREET, AND 88, 90, 92, 94, 96, 98, 100 JOHNSON-STREET,
BROOKLYN, EASTERN DISTRICT.

1856.

Cover page of the Starr, Fellows and Company Illustrated 1856 Catalogue of Lamps and Gas Fixtures.

Circular.

Dear Sir:

The co-partnership heretofore existing under the name and style of **STARR, FELLOWS & CO.** *expired by limitation on the first of February, 1857.*

WM. H. STARR, *so long and so favorably known as the head of the house, having sold his interest therein to the remaining partners, and they having associated with themselves* **Mr. J. A. G. COMSTOCK,** *the business will be continued as heretofore, at the same locality, under the name and style of* FELLOWS, HOFFMAN & CO.

The new firm will endeavor to deserve the liberal share of confidence and friendship this house has hitherto enjoyed in the commercial community.

CHAS. H. FELLOWS,
CHAS. O. HOFFMAN,
JER. A. G. COMSTOCK,
JAS. G. DOLBEARE,
GEO. NICHOLS.

74 BEEKMAN STREET,

New York, March 2d, 1857.

A circular from the catalogue dated March 2, 1857, indicating that Mr. Starr has sold his interest in the business and the firm's name has changed to Fellows, Hoffman and Company.

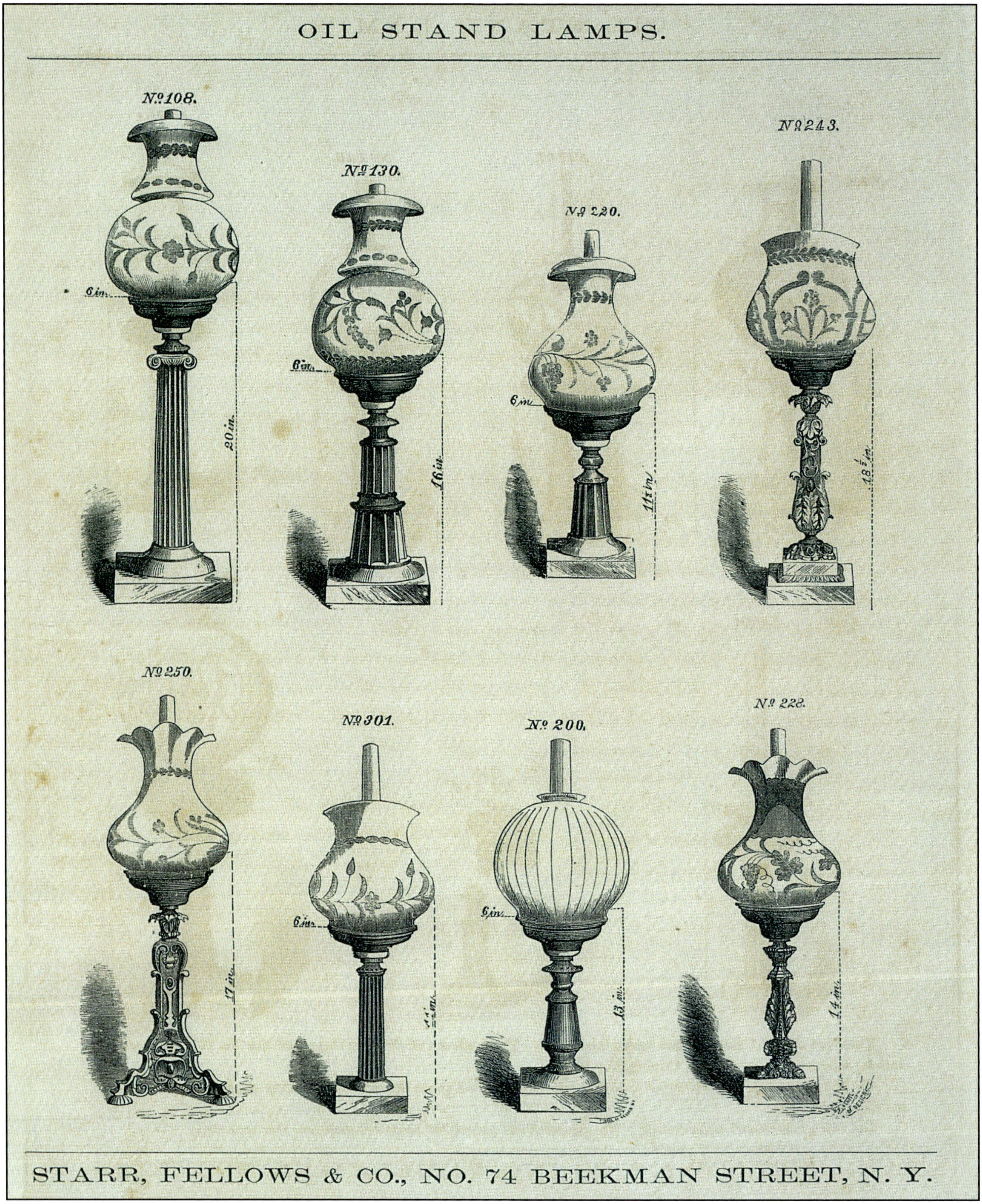

Page from the 1856 Starr, Fellows and Company catalogue depicting a variety of different styles of solar stand lamps. In the catalogue, solar lamps are referred to as "Oil Stand Lamps."

OIL STAND LAMPS.

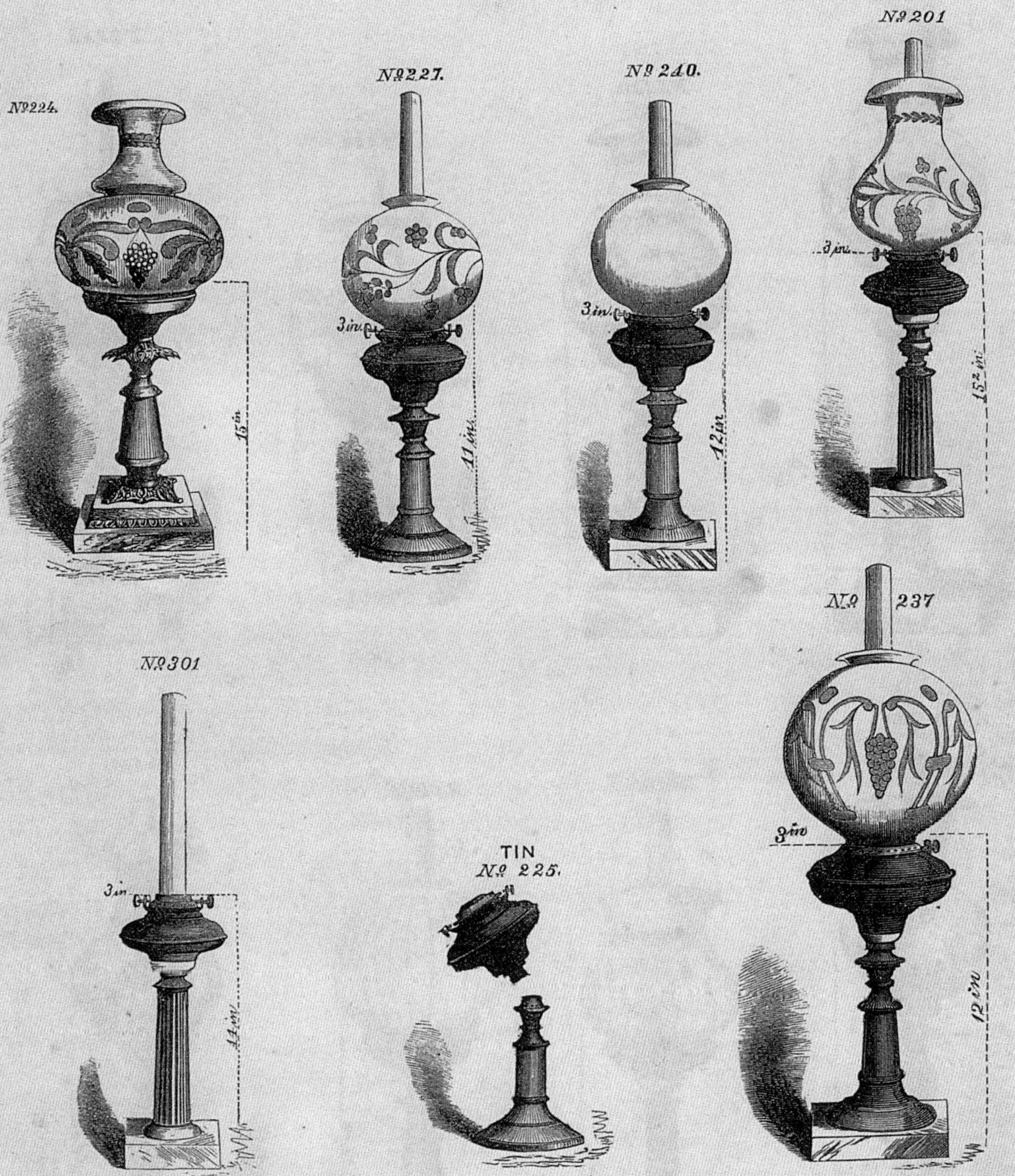

These are all No. 1 Burners, and take a 3 in. Globe. The heads are all the same shape, and like No. 237. The artist in drawing followed his own fancy in shaping them.

No. 237 is drawn on a much larger scale than the others, as will be readily seen by comparing the figures which indicate the different heights.

No. 225 is represented as unscrewed. When papered and packed, the heads and stands are thus separated.

STARR, FELLOWS & CO., NO. 74 BEEKMAN STREET, N. Y.

Another page from the Starr, Fellows and Company 1856 catalogue, illustrating an additional series of solar lamps. Many of the lamps shown have globes that sit directly atop the burner or so-called "top mount." All top mount globes in lamps equipped with No. 1 burners have a 3" diameter fitter.

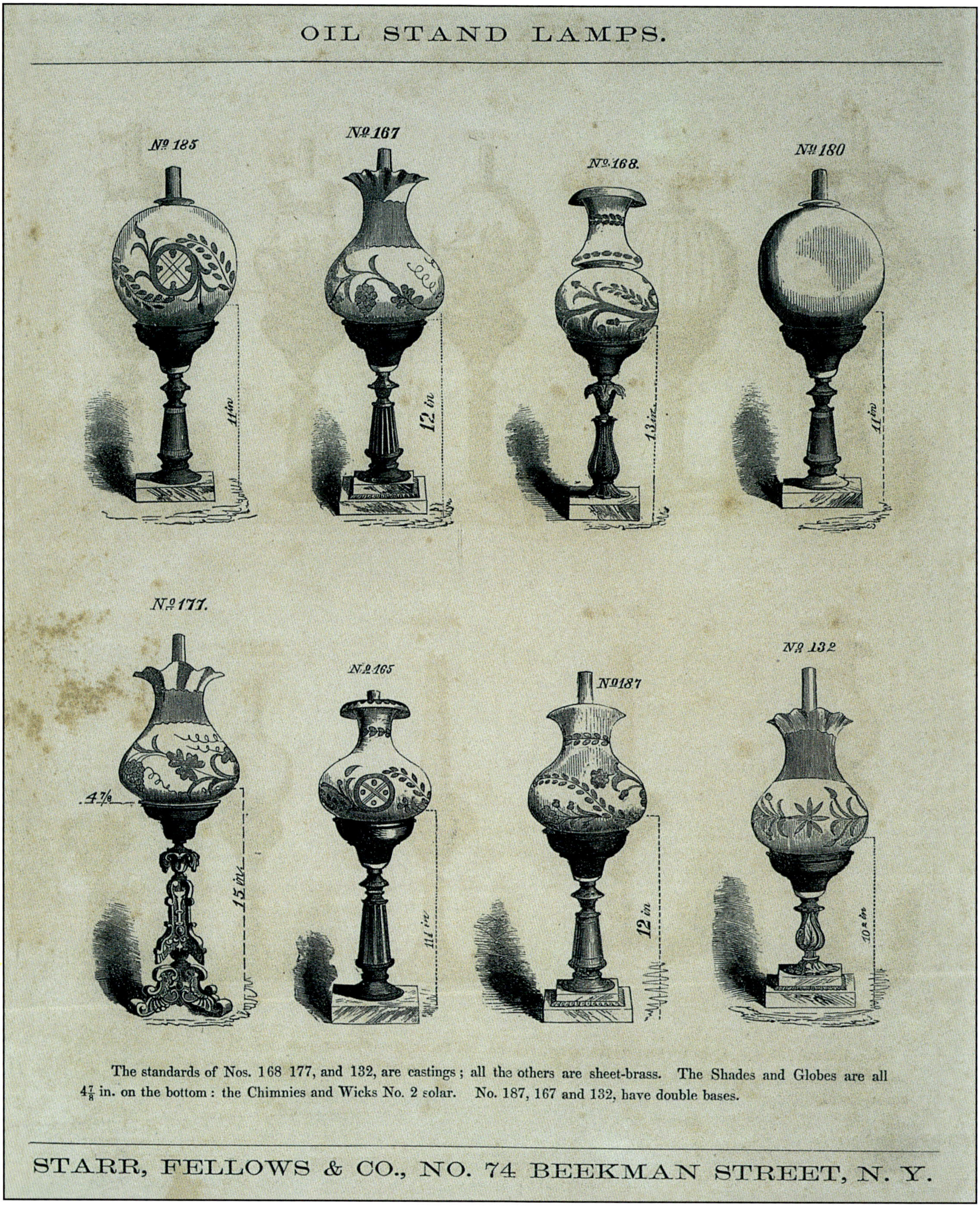
OIL STAND LAMPS.

The standards of Nos. 168 177, and 132, are castings; all the others are sheet-brass. The Shades and Globes are all $4\frac{7}{8}$ in. on the bottom: the Chimnies and Wicks No. 2 solar. No. 187, 167 and 132, have double bases.

STARR, FELLOWS & CO., NO. 74 BEEKMAN STREET, N. Y.

Another page from the Starr, Fellows and Company 1856 catalogue, showing a variety of solar lamp styles with all globes resting upon the shade rings.

OIL STAND LAMPS.

Nos. 155 and 181 have 4⅞ in. Globes; all the others, with No. 144 tin, on the following page, take 2½ in. Globes, and all No. 2 Solar Chimnies. The Standards to 155, 131 and 178, are castings; the latter being unscrewed to show where the heads and stands are separated.

STARR, FELLOWS & CO., NO. 74 BEEKMAN STREET, N. Y.

Variety of solar lamps from the Starr, Fellows and Company 1856 catalogue. Note that all top mounted globes in lamps equipped with No. 2 burners have a 2.5" diameter fitter.

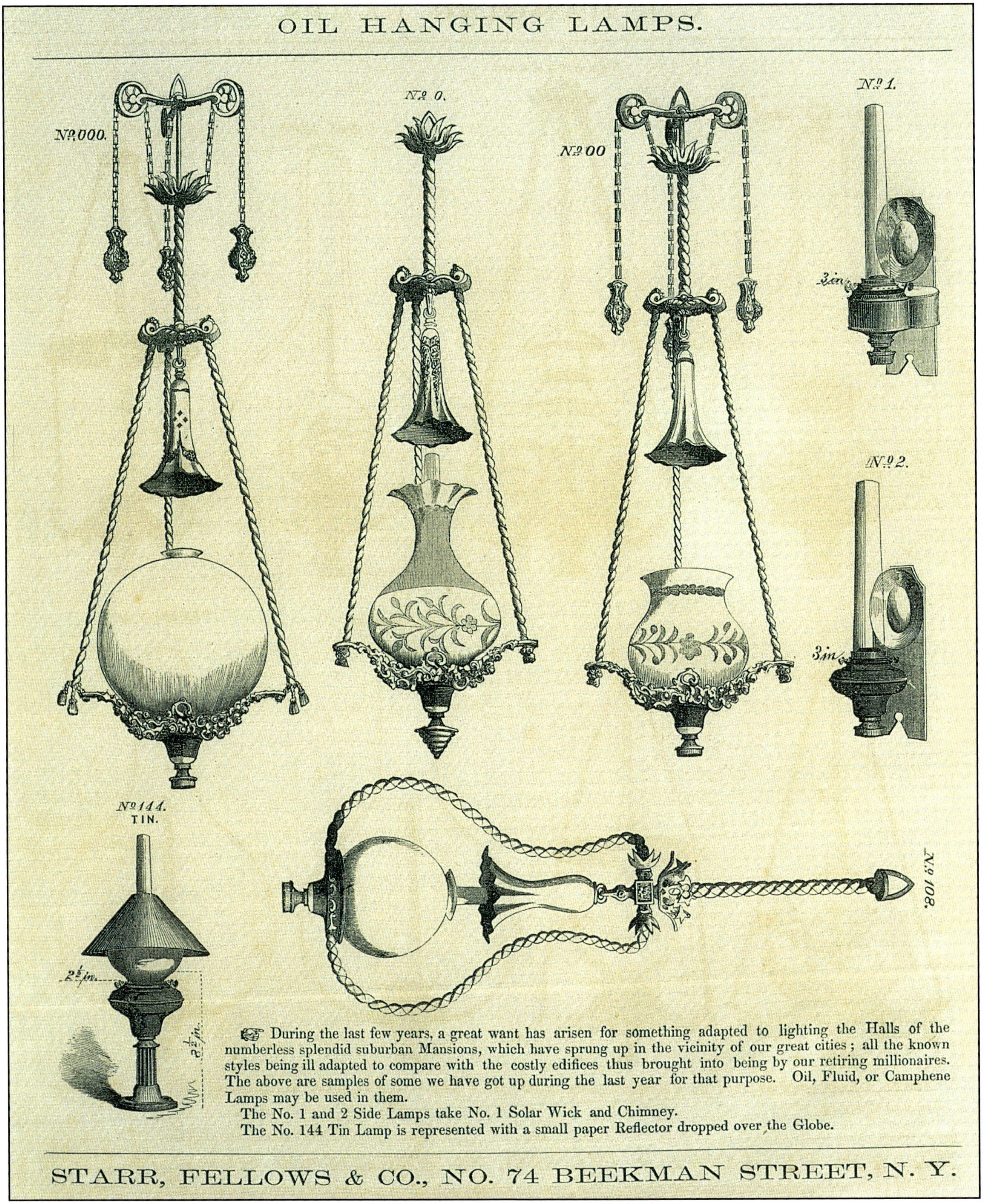

OIL HANGING LAMPS.

No. 000.

No. 0.

No. 00

No. 1.

3 in.

No. 2.

3 in.

No. 144.
TIN.

$2\frac{1}{2}$ in.

$8\frac{1}{2}$ in.

No. 108.

☞ During the last few years, a great want has arisen for something adapted to lighting the Halls of the numberless splendid suburban Mansions, which have sprung up in the vicinity of our great cities; all the known styles being ill adapted to compare with the costly edifices thus brought into being by our retiring millionaires. The above are samples of some we have got up during the last year for that purpose. Oil, Fluid, or Camphene Lamps may be used in them.

The No. 1 and 2 Side Lamps take No. 1 Solar Wick and Chimney.

The No. 144 Tin Lamp is represented with a small paper Reflector dropped over the Globe.

STARR, FELLOWS & CO., NO. 74 BEEKMAN STREET, N. Y.

Illustrations from the 1856 Starr, Fellows and Company catalogue of hanging lamps and wall sconces that utilize oil, burning fluid, or camphene.

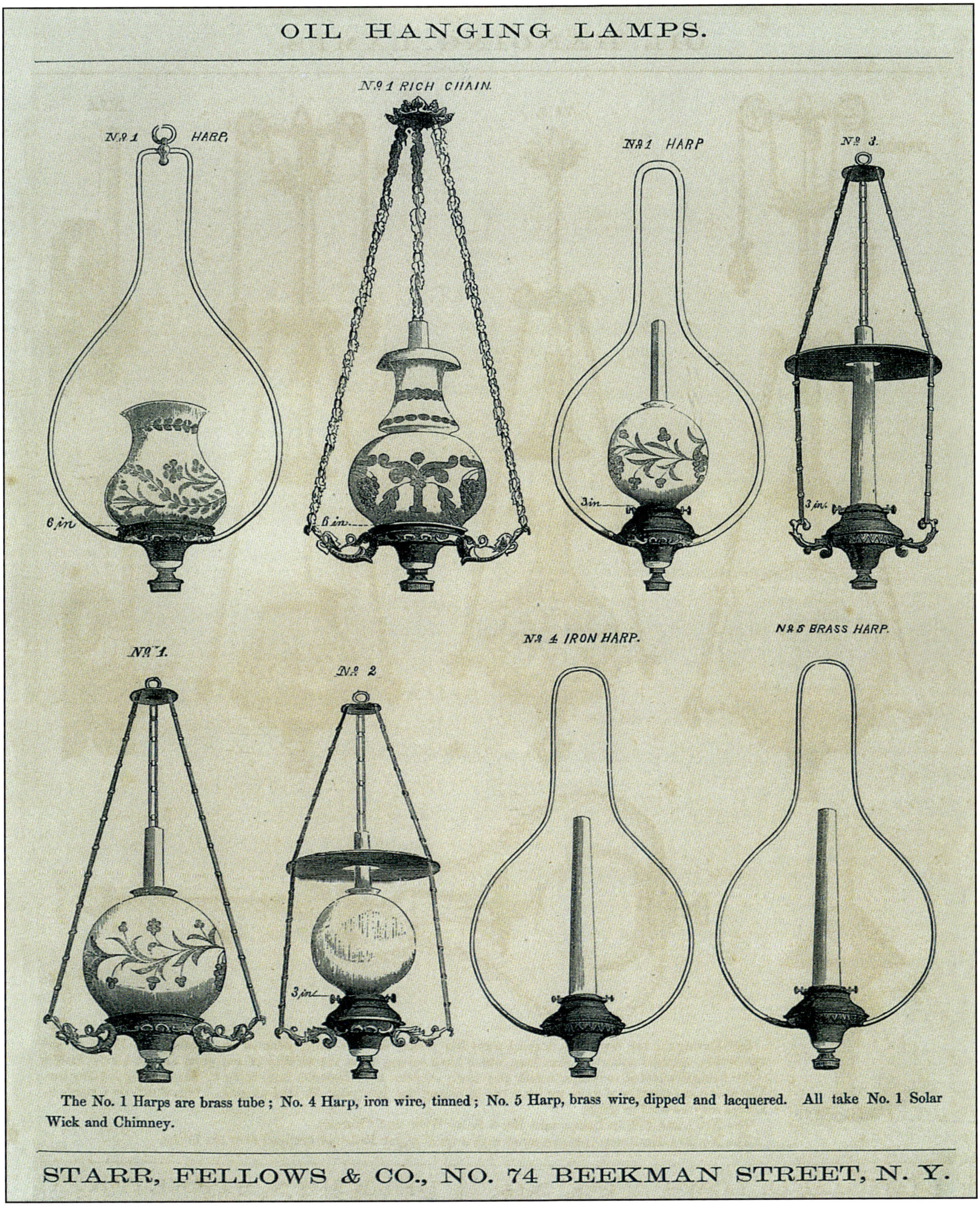

OIL HANGING LAMPS.

The No. 1 Harps are brass tube; No. 4 Harp, iron wire, tinned; No. 5 Harp, brass wire, dipped and lacquered. All take No. 1 Solar Wick and Chimney.

STARR, FELLOWS & CO., NO. 74 BEEKMAN STREET, N. Y.

Illustrations from the 1856 Starr, Fellows and Company catalogue of oil (solar) hanging lamps suspended from harps or chains.

Gilt lacquered brass and bronze solar lamp, a form rarely seen, attributed to Starr, Fellows and Company, c. 1850. The design is illustrated in their 1856 catalogue as item No. 178. A bulbous cut and etched blown glass shade with a faceted neck is supported by a font containing a No. 2 burner dated 1853. Snowflake crystal pendants are suspended from the shade ring. In original condition. Height to the shade ring: 11". Overall height: 20". $1,800-$2,200.

Gilt lacquered brass and bronze solar lamp attributed to Starr, Fellows and Company, c. 1850, and identified as item No. 165 in their 1856 catalogue. The ball form cut and etched blown glass shade has a 5" diameter fitter and rests on a font containing a No. 2 burner. The fluted standard is raised on a square marble plinth. In original condition. Height to the shade ring: 12.375". Overall height: 21". $1,200-$1,800.

Gilt lacquered brass and bronze solar lamp attributed to Starr, Fellows and Company, c. 1850. The same lamp is illustrated in their 1856 catalogue as items No. 168 (solar), 205 (camphene), and 268 (burning fluid). The bulbous cut and etched blown glass shade is decorated with berries, has a rolled rim, and a 5" diameter fitter. The font contains a No. 1 burner. The beaded standard is raised on a double marble plinth divided by a foliated border. In original condition. Height to the shade ring: 12". Overall height: 20". $1,800-$2,200.

Gilt lacquered brass hanging burning fluid lamp attributed to Starr, Fellows and Company, c. 1850, and shown in their 1856 catalogue as item No. 1. A harp supports the font. A dainty cut and etched glass smoke bell is suspended over the etched and cut blown glass shade. In original condition. Overall height: 25.75". $4,000-$4,500.

Gilt lacquered brass and bronze solar lamp attributed to Starr, Fellows and Company, c. 1850, and found in their 1856 catalogue as item No. 250. The unusual bulbous cut and etched blown glass shade has a waisted and faceted neck and rolled rim. The shade is decorated with Maltese crosses contained within circles. The 6" shade ring supports snowflake crystal pendants that were probably supplied by Sandwich Glass Company. The triangular standard is raised on button feet. This standard is also illustrated in the 1850 Hooper catalogue (without feet) as item No. 636. In original condition. Height to the shade ring: 14.5". Overall height: 26". $4,500-$5,500.

Gilt lacquered brass and bronze solar lamp attributed to Starr, Fellows and Company, c. 1850, and illustrated in their 1856 catalogue as item No. 132. The bulbous cut and etched blown glass "Oregon" style shade with ruffled rim is decorated with geometric motifs and has a 5" wide fitter. The font contains a No. 2 burner. The standard is raised on a double marble plinth. In original condition. Height to the shade ring: 10". Overall height: 19". $1,000-$1,500.

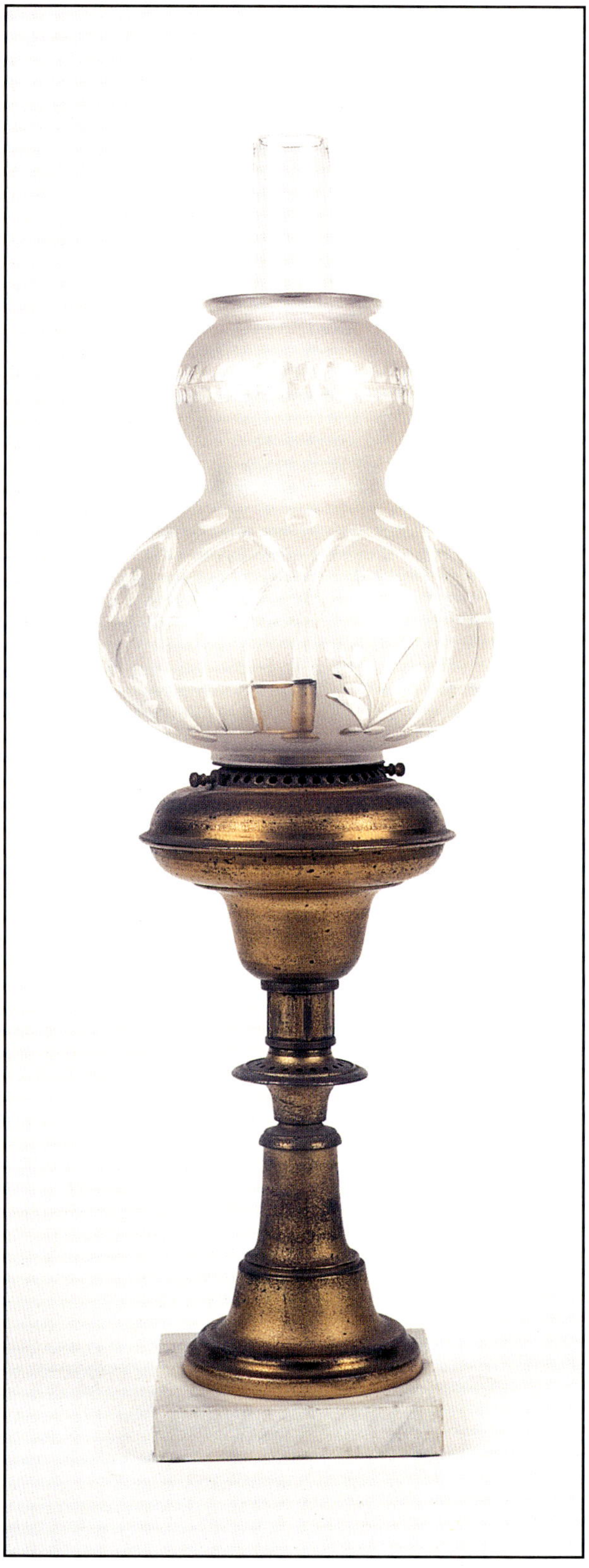

Gilt lacquered brass and bronze solar lamp attributed to Starr, Fellows and Company, c. 1850 and identified in their 1856 catalogue as item No. 237. The unusual turban form cut and etched blown glass shade has a 3" wide fitter and rests directly on the No. 1 burner (top mount). The shade is decorated with gothic motifs. The standard is atop a square marble plinth. In original condition. Height to the shade ring: 10.5". Overall height: 21.5". $2,200-$3,000.

Gilt lacquered brass and bronze solar lamp attributed to Starr, Fellows and Company, c. 1850, and depicted in their 1856 catalogue as item No. 250. The cut and etched blown glass shade is ornamented by vines, has a faceted neck, and a rolled rim. The font contains a No. 1 burner. The standard is virtually the same as found in the 1850 Hooper catalogue, item No. 660. The surface is restored. Height to the shade ring: 16.5". Overall height: 28". $1,800-$2,200.

Gilt lacquered brass and bronze solar lamp attributed to Starr, Fellows and Company, c. 1850, and identified as item No. 130 in their 1856 catalogue. Gothic arches decorate the ball form cut and etched blown glass shade having a 6" wide fitter. The font is equipped with a No. 1 burner. The tapered reeded standard is raised on a square marble plinth. The surface is restored. Height to the shade ring: 14.5". Overall height: 22.25". $1,800-$2,200.

Gilt lacquered brass hanging solar lamp attributed to Starr, Fellows and Company, c.1850, and depicted in their 1856 catalogue as items No. 4 (iron harp) and 5 (brass harp). The catalogue illustrations are shown without globes or pendants. In this example, a ball form cut and etched blown glass globe sits atop the font. The periphery of the font is decorated with flowers from which snowflake pendants are suspended. In original condition. Overall length: 25". $4,500-$5,000.

Gilt lacquered brass and bronze solar lamp attributed to Starr, Fellows and Company, c. 1850, and identified as item No. 177 in their 1856 catalogue. The finely cut and etched blown glass shade displays a wedding ring design and has a 5" diameter fitter. The font is equipped with a No. 2 burner. Leaves, cartouches, and cabochons ornament the standard. The triangular plinth terminates in scroll feet. The shade ring supports 6" crystal tapered Albert pendants. In original condition. Height to the shade ring: 12.375". Overall height: 21". $1,800-$2,500.

Gilt lacquered and patinated brass and bronze solar lamp attributed to Starr, Fellows and Company, c. 1850. The ball form cut and etched blown glass globe is decorated with vines and berries and has a 5" fitter. The font contains a No. 2 burner. The fluted standard rests on a square marble plinth. This lamp is nearly identical to one illustrated in the 1856 Starr, Fellows and Company catalogue as item No. 301. In original condition. Height to the shade ring: 12.25". Overall height: 19". $550-$900.

Chapter Three

The Dietz Companies

Robert Edwin Dietz (1818-1897), an ambitious young man of twenty-two years, set up his first lamp and oil business at 5 Hicks Street in Brooklyn, New York, in 1840. Shortly thereafter, Robert took on two partners: his brother, William Henry Dietz, and John A. Weed. In 1843, they opened a lamp shop at 13 John Street in Manhattan. The partnership name became Dietz, Brother and Company and it first appears as such in the 1844-45 New York City Directory. The firm probably produced its own brass castings but purchased glassware from other manufacturers. Numerous solar lamps were generated but Dietz-made Argand and sinumbra lamps have not been identified.

As the business expanded to one of the largest in the United States, it acquired a factory and shop at 139 William Street in 1847.

By 1849, the Dietz company had entered into a relationship with the Philadelphia firm of Cornelius and Company and was selling the latter's "celebrated Patent Solar Lard Lamp." Also, about this same time, there is evidence suggesting that the Dietz Company was not only a retail supplier but a wholesaler of metal castings to such firms as Starr, Fellows and Company.

From 1850 to 1855, the firm suffered a number of ups and downs culminating in its closure in 1855. Prior to its closure, the firm marked some of its wares with an inscribed brass plate soldered to the font that read: "Dietz, Brother & Co. New York." Sometimes the address of 139 William Street was included in the inscription.

The business reopened in 1856 and at that time was known as Dietz and Company. In general, the products of Dietz and Company were rarely marked from this time forward.

By 1860, the firm was again soundly established and concentrating on kerosene burning lamps. That year, both Robert Edwin and his younger brother, Michael Dietz, received patents for kerosene burners.

Over the next several years, the firm initially prospered but later struggled and began to fragment. A London branch was established in 1860 and maintained by Michael. Robert Edwin pursued the manufacturing of tubular lanterns. Finally, in 1875 Dietz and Company's New York office closed for good.

Robert Edwin continued in the lantern business until his death in 1897 at the age of seventy-nine years.

In 1860, an illustrated catalogue was published; a few of its plates depicting solar lamps are shown on the following pages.

Front cover of the reproduction 1860 Dietz and Company Illustrated Catalogue.

Z & COMPANY,

ESTABLISHED 1840.

ATED CATALOGUE.

ILDINGS, LITTLE CARTER LANE, LONDON, E. C.

4 WILLIAM STREET, NEW YORK, U. S. A.

Plate 32 from the 1860 Dietz and Company Catalogue depicting numerous solar lamps.

Plate 33, item No. 52 from the 1860 Dietz catalogue. Note that this lamp including the globe is identical to that in the next illustration.

Labeled Dietz, Brother and Company gilt lacquered brass and bronze solar lamp relating to an example illustrated in the Dietz catalogue of 1860, Plate 33, item No. 52 (shown on page 119). This is the most ornate solar lamp produced by the Dietz Company. The ball form cut and etched blown glass shade with gothic decorations and a 6" wide fitter is identical to the one shown in the catalogue. The font retains its original burner components. The standard is designed from elements of gothic architecture and sits atop a hexagonal plinth. The second casting from the base is signed: "T C Salt," a Birmingham, England lamp manufacturer. The surface is restored. Height to the shade ring: 22.5". Overall height: 31". $5,000-$6,000.

Detail of manufacturer's label from the previous solar lamp.

Gilt lacquered brass and bronze solar lamp attributed to Dietz, c. 1850. This lamp is illustrated on Plate 32, item No. 153 in the 1860 Dietz and Company catalogue. The elaborately cut and etched "Oregon" style blown glass shade has a 5" diameter fitter and rests on a font containing its original burner. The bulbous standard is raised on a double marble plinth. In original condition. Height to the shade ring: 12.75". Overall height: 23.25". $1,200-$1,800.

Labeled Dietz, Brother and Company gilt lacquered and patinated bronze and brass solar lamp, c. 1850, relating to Plate 32, item No. 199 in the 1860 Dietz catalogue. The bulbous form cut and etched blown glass globe has a 6" fitter and rests on a font that retains its original burner elements. The unusual standard incorporates gothic and rococo motifs. Hanging from the shade ring are back-cut Albert pendants. The surface has been restored. Height to the shade ring: 15". Overall height: 25.75". $1,800-$2,200.

Labeled Dietz, Brother and Company gilt lacquered brass and bronze solar lamp, c. 1850. It relates to Plate 32, item No. 54 in the 1860 Dietz catalogue. The cut and etched blown glass shade has a 2.5" fitter resting directly on the burner (top mount). The font is raised on a fluted columnar standard above a square marble plinth. In original condition. Height to the font: 9.5". Overall height: 16.75". $1,000-$1,500.

Labeled Dietz, Brother and Company gilt lacquered brass and bronze solar lamp, c. 1850, relating to Plate 32, item No. 210 in the 1860 Dietz catalogue. The label is one used up to 1855. The ball form cut and etched blown glass shade displays crosses within circles and has a 6" wide fitter. The font contains a factory fitted burner and is raised on a Corinthian topped reeded columnar standard. The octagonal pedestal rests on a square marble plinth. The surface is restored. Height to the shade ring: 18.5". Overall height: 27". $2,500-$3,500.

Detail of label from the previous solar lamp. It reads: "Dietz Brother & Company New York," indicating production up to 1855.

Gilt lacquered brass and lacquered brass solar lamp attributed to Dietz, c. 1850, and depicted in their 1860 catalogue on Plate 32 as item No. 122 (on a different base). The font contains an original burner. The standard is in the form of a female figure carrying a basket in her right arm with her left arm on a tree stump, while she stands on a columnar base atop a square plinth. The unusual form cut and etched blown glass shade has an everted neck, a 5" diameter fitter, and a rolled rim. The surface is restored. Height to the shade ring: 12.75". Overall height: 23.75". $2,500-$3,000.

Detail of figural standard seen in previous lamp.

Labeled Dietz, Brother and Company gilt lacquered brass and bronze solar lamp, c. 1850. It relates to Plate 32, item No. 164 in the 1860 Dietz catalogue and is also shown as item No. 627 in the Hooper catalogue of 1850 (see page 42). The bulbous cut and etched blown glass shade is ornamented with vines and has a rolled rim above a faceted neck. The shade fitter diameter is 6". The font is equipped with its original burner components. The standard is in the form of an iris in bloom. A border of leaves divides the double square marble plinth. Suspended from the shade ring are "C" pendants, usually found on higher quality solar lamps. The surface is restored. Height to the shade ring: 15". Overall height: 25.25". $2,200-$3,000.

Gilt lacquered brass three light girandole, c. 1850, relating to one illustrated in the 1860 Dietz catalogue on page 17, figure 11. The reverse side of the girandole is stamped: "12-18-49." The standard is modeled after the Cathedral in Mount Auburn Cemetery, Cambridge, Massachusetts. The author has seen other models of the same design stamped: "W F Shaw Boston."

Chapter Four

The Messenger Companies

Thomas Messenger, brass founder, was born September 19, 1767 and resided at Hall Field House (also called Hall Hill House) on Wellington Road, Edgbaston, England. He and his wife, Sarah, had several children, including three sons: Thomas Henry (1798-1811), Samuel (1805-1868), and Alfred (1808-1824). Thomas Henry and Alfred died at ages thirteen and sixteen years respectively, leaving Samuel as the only son to reach adulthood.

Birmingham, England has a long history of metalworking, and manufacturing was quite prominent in this city at the beginning of the nineteenth century.

The brass foundry of Thomas Messenger and Thomas Phipson made its first appearance in the Birmingham City Directory in 1797. Their address at that time was Park Street.

By 1800, the firm had moved to Loveday Street and occupied that address for the next several years. Little is known about the early life of the business.

An 1808 advertisement in an English trade directory lists Messenger and Phipson as: "Brass Founders, Manufacturers of Church Candlesticks, Patent Lamps, Etc." Broad Street in Birmingham is given as their address.

At some point during the war against France (1793-1815), the firm employed up to 250 workers, making it one of the larger brass companies in Birmingham. By contrast, the majority of the metal companies were small factories employing 20-30 workers. Coinciding with an economic depression, the company's workforce dropped to around 100 in the year 1812. At that time, the firm paid its "best men" £3 per week, which was substantially higher than several other similar manufacturers.

In 1822, Robson's Directory has Messenger and Phipson located at 21 Greville Street, London.

1823 is the last year Messenger and Phipson appear in the Birmingham City Directory; their location is given as 22 Broad Street, Birmingham. That same year an advertisement lists the Messenger and Phipson's London address as 20 Greville Street.

The Robson's 1826 and 1827 City of London Directory lists Thomas Messenger as a: "Lamp Manufacturer." His address is 20 & 21 Greville Street, Hatton Garden. Phipson is no longer mentioned in association with Messenger.

The following year, the firm of Messenger and Son is first described. The author's research concludes that Thomas's son, Samuel, at age twenty-three, was brought into the firm at or about this time.

The 20 Greville Street address is found in the London Directory of 1826 and appears in the Post Office Records until 1832.

For the next seventeen years, the Hatton Garden address, sometimes with the street number of 63, is the sole London location listed.

The 1830 Birmingham and London City Directories classify the firm of Thomas Messenger and Son as: "Brass Founders and Lamp and Lantern Manufacturers."

On October 27, 1832, at age sixty-five, Thomas Messenger died, leaving his only surviving son, Samuel, age twenty-seven, the head of the business. After Thomas's death, the firm's name was changed from Messenger and Son to Messenger and Sons (plural). The significance of the name change is unclear.

By 1833, the business known as Messenger and Sons became the first of several English firms to specialize in gas light fixtures.

A trade card, c. 1835, of Thomas Messenger and Sons describes the firm as: "Manufacturers of Chandeliers, Tripods and Lamps of Every Description in Bronze and Or-Molu." The firm applied a plethora of classical designs, utilizing illustrations from the Italian architect Giovanni Battista Piranesi (1720-1778). Piranesi was a Venetian, who could not find sufficient work in Rome and therefore produced etchings. Over a forty year period, his work yielded some of the most vividly detailed and occasionally fantasized images of the modern and ancient city of Rome[1]. In 1778, he published *Vasi, Candelabri, Cippi, Scarcofugi, Tripod, Lucerne, Ornamenti Antichi*, a collection of etchings that are rich in classical depictions of Roman oil lamps and other artifacts.

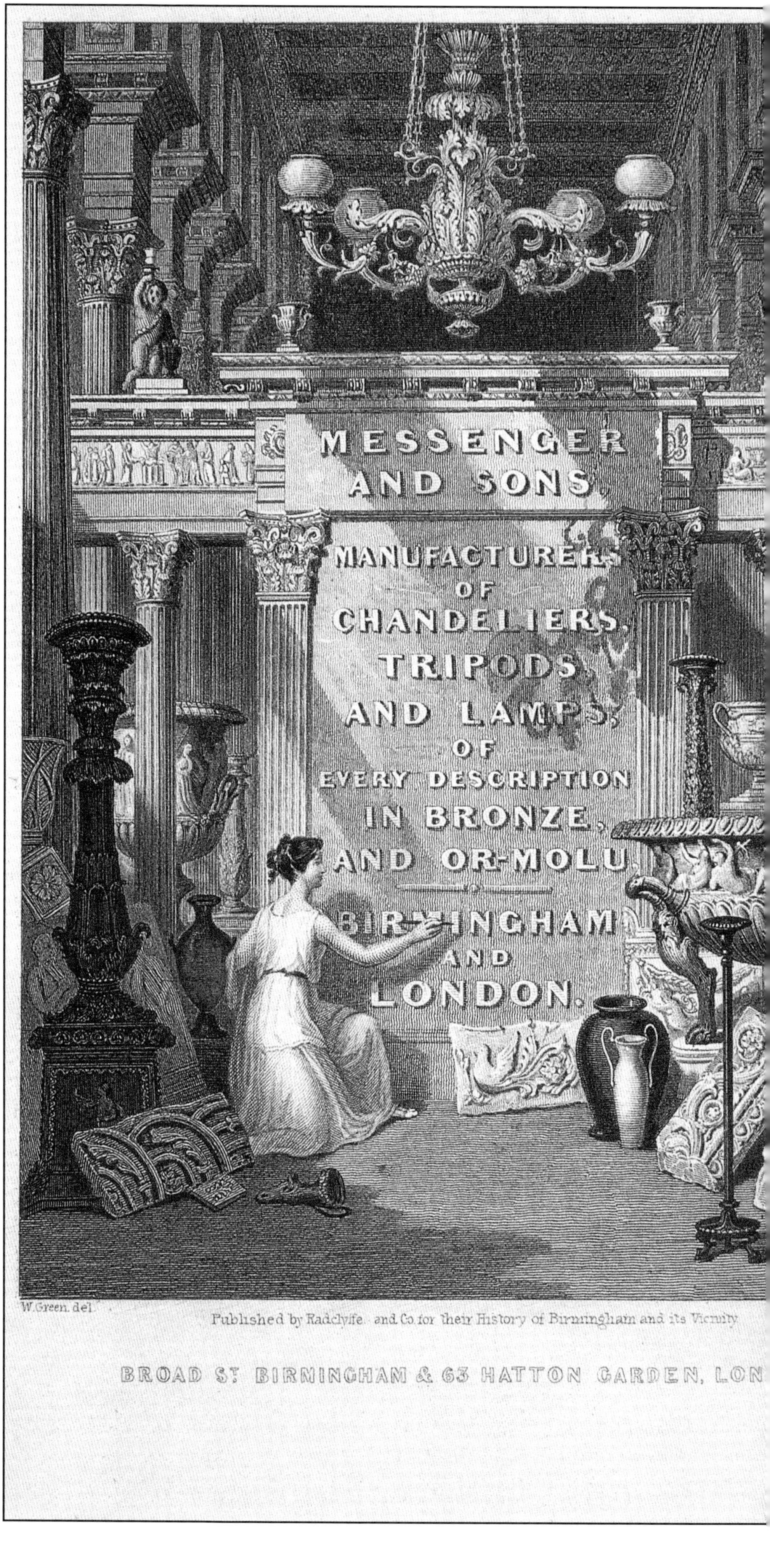

Beautifully illustrated Messenger and Sons trade card advertisement, c. 1835. The advertisement reads: "Messenger and Sons Manufacturers of Chandeliers, Tripods and Lamps, of Every Description In Bronze, And Or-molu Birmingham and London." The caption beneath the illustration reads: "Broad St. Birmingham & 63 Hatton Garden, London." *Courtesy of Birmingham Museum and Art Gallery.*

The Messenger Company frequently borrowed from Piranesi's etchings when designing their lighting devices. Argand fuel reservoirs were patterned after a Roman funeral monument. Other Messenger lamps used the Three Graces as a standard. Paw feet were common.

Three pairs of Argand lamps were purchased from the Birmingham Messenger location by the Duke of Newcastle in 1838. A rhyton was incorporated into the design of these lamps.

In 1849, Messenger and Sons' London location is listed as 73 Hatton Garden in the city directory.

The 1850 city directories give the Birmingham address as 15 and 16 Broad Street. Also, that same year the Birmingham Directory describes the firm as: "Manufacturers of Chandeliers, Lamps, Candelabras, Plain and Ornamental Brass Iron Bedsteads, Pattern Railway Signals, Carriage, Roof and Side Lamps and General Artificers."

Samuel Messenger received patents for improvements in certain lamps and gas fittings in 1853 and 1857.

With the decline of heavy oils as a lighting fuel and the discovery of kerosene, the Messenger firm switched to the then more modern combustibles in their lighting products. The firm displayed a wide range of lighting fixtures in classical and gothic tastes at the 1862 International Exhibition.

Addressing Messenger and other manufacturers' superior artistic interpretation and application to designs in the lighting industry is the following, taken from an 1866 Report for the British Association:

> The trade is one which claims to...kept alive a superior class of workmen, in which proportions of the remains of classical moulding...were used and in which pillars (sic) Corinthian, Ionic, Composite, etc...supported lamps, or caryatid figures bent under the imaginary weight of the lamp they were supposed to sustain. One designer represented 'Atlas supporting an improved brass Liverpool lamp' with arms extended, hands pressed on stomach, the lamp apparently balanced on his head...Probably nothing more instructional as to progress in the direction of applied design can possibly be gathered than by turning over the pages of the pattern books of the Messengers...of a by-gone period[2].

So pattern books of the Messenger Company existed in 1866 and may be available today if someone had the time, means, and knowledge of where to search. If found, they would truly be an important, historical treasure.

Messenger made kerosene lamps utilizing "Duplex" burners after the Hinks 1865 patent expired.

The firm continued to produce lighting products into the twentieth century. There is even a catalogue, c. 1908, that describes electric fittings. In the 1920s, the firm was absorbed into the Veritas House (Falk, Stadelman, Ltd.) and is no longer in business today.

Messenger lighting wares were frequently but not consistently marked by the manufacturer. The outside of the cast iron plate in the plinth of Argand, sinumbra, and solar lamps is sometimes stamped: "Messenger." The firm's name, along with the phrase "Published as the Act Directs," may be found cast into the underside of the iron plate. This quotation refers to an English law and its amendments, dated May 18, 1814, which stated: "An Act for encouraging the Art of making new models and casts of busts...any new and original sculpture...of the Human figure...Animal or any animal combined with Human figure." The act granted exclusive right to its use for fourteen years provided the maker placed his name and date on each piece.

Often soldered to the burner tube of Argand and sinumbra lamps are brass plates bearing the firm's name and address, sometimes above that of the retailer.

The following chronology obtained from the Birmingham and Robson's London City Directories and London Post Office Records may be of some help to the reader in dating Messenger lighting wares:

Messenger Time Line

Year	Firm Name	Address	City	Advertising
1797	Messenger and Phipson	Park Street	Birmingham	Brass Founders
1800	Messenger and Phipson	Loveday Street	Birmingham	
1801	Messenger and Phipson	Loveday Street	Birmingham	
1803	Messenger and Phipson	Loveday Street	Birmingham	
1805	Messenger and Phipson	Loveday Street	Birmingham	
1808	Messenger and Phipson	Broad Street	Birmingham	Brass Founders, Manufacturers of Church Candle sticks, Patent Lamps, Etc.
1815	Messenger and Phipson	Broad Street	Birmingham	
1818	Messenger and Phipson	Broad Street	Birmingham	
1821	Messenger and Phipson	Broad Street	Birmingham	Brass Founders, Lamp Manufacturers
1822	Messenger and Phipson	21 Greville Street, Hatton Garden	London	Lamp Manufacturer
1823	Messenger and Phipson	22 Broad Street	Birmingham	
1823	Messenger and Phipson	20 Greville Street	London	
1826	Thomas Messenger	20 & 21 Greville Street, Hatton Garden	London	
1827	Thomas Messenger	20 & 21 Greville Street	London	
1828	Thomas Messenger & Son	20 Greville Street	London	Lamp Manufacturers
1829	Thomas Messenger & Son	20 Greville Street	London	Lamp Manufacturers
1830	Thomas Messenger & Son	Broad Street	Birmingham	
1830	Thomas Messenger & Son	20 Greville Street, Hatton Garden	London	Brass Founders, Lamp, Lantern Manufacturers
1831	Thomas Messenger & Son	20 Greville Street	London	Lamp Manufacturers
1832	Thomas Messenger & Sons	20 Greville Street	London	Lamp Manufacturers
1833	Thomas Messenger & Sons	63 Hatton Garden	London	
1834	Thomas Messenger & Sons	63 Hatton Garden	London	Lamp Manufacturers
1835	Thomas Messenger & Sons	22 Broad Street	Birmingham	
1835	Thomas Messenger & Sons	63 Hatton Garden	London	Brass Founders
1836	Thomas Messenger & Sons	63 Hatton Garden	London	Lamp Manufacturers
1837	Thomas Messenger & Sons	63 Hatton Garden	London	
1838-48	Thomas Messenger & Sons	63 Hatton Garden	London	Lamp & Chandelier Manufacturing
1849	Thomas Messenger & Sons	73 Hatton Garden	London	Lamp Manufacturing
1850	Messenger & Sons	15 & 16 Broad Street	Birmingham	
1850	Messenger & Sons	73 Hatton Garden	London	Manufacturers of Chandeliers, Lamps & Candlelabras, Plain and Ornamental Brass Bedsteads, Patent Railway Signal, Carriage Roof & Side Lamps & General Artificers
1851-61	Messenger & Sons	73 Hatton Garden	London	
1908	Messenger & Sons	Electric Fittings and others		
1920s	Messenger	Bought out by Veritas Company		

[1]Helen Dudar, "The Grandeur That Was Rome," *Smithsonian,* Vol. 31, No. 1, April, 2000, pgs. 87-88.

[2]Leeds City Art Gallery, *Country House Lighting,* Leeds, England, 1992, pgs. 81-82.

Elegant signed pair of gilt lacquered brass and bronze single light Argand lamps, early second quarter nineteenth century. Labels affixed to the cylindrical standards read: "Messenger and Sons 20 Greville Street London & Birmingham." The spread eagles bear an inscription that reads "M and P," denoting the earlier Messenger and Phipson Company. Urn shaped fonts are embellished with applied arabesque festoons and masks of Bacchus, the Roman god of wine. The eagles are raised on a foliated socle surmounted on an octagonal plinth. The beautifully etched and cut blown glass shades depict lyres interspersed with geometric designs. The shade necks and rims are faceted. The surfaces have been restored. Overall height: 18.25". $25,000-$30,000 for the pair.

Signed pair of patinated bronze and brass sinumbra lamps, second quarter nineteenth century. Stamped on the cast iron base weight is: "Published As The Act Directs Messenger & Sons London." The foliated embossed 10" diameter shade rings support cut and etched blown glass globes decorated with double dove designs. The fonts are flat, having no curved mold to their configuration. The foliated and reeded drip cups surmount the heavens, which—according to Greek mythology—Atlas is condemned to bear the weight of upon his shoulders. Masks, possibly the Four Winds, floral embellishments, and wreathes adorn the octagonal base and plinth. Lamps with similar bases and standards are shown on pages 136, 139, 153, and 208. In original condition. Height to the shade ring: 24". Overall height: 33.5". $25,000-$30,000 for the pair.

Detail of the unusually shaped font seen in previous lamp. The painted surface of this font is relatively flat. Most sinumbra fonts demonstrate significant curvature in this area.

Signed brass sinumbra lamp, second quarter nineteenth century. The cast iron base weight is stamped: "Messenger." The 10" shade ring supports a cut and etched blown glass globe with leaf and berry designs. The floral stenciled cylindrical standard is raised on a double stepped square plinth. In original condition. Height to the shade ring: 20". Overall height: 28.5". $9,000-$10,000.

A patinated bronze single light Argand lamp in the form of a classical rhyton, attributed to Messenger and Sons, second quarter nineteenth century. The design of this lamp is patterned after the Piranesi etching of a Roman monument. The cone shaped finial and fuel valve adjustment handle sit atop the urn shaped font. Emerging from the mouth of the acanthi embellished boar is the burner that supports a cut and etched trumpet style glass globe decorated with floral motifs. A scalloped handle is attached to the font. According to *Country House Lighting*, pg. 145 (see Bibliography), in 1838, the Duke of Newcastle purchased from Messenger and Sons three sets of rhyton-figured lamps, nearly identical to the one seen here. In original condition. Height to the finial: 7". $2,500-$3,500.

Gilt lacquered brass and bronze sinumbra lamp bearing the label of Messenger and Sons, second quarter nineteenth century. The cut and etched blown glass shade is decorated with lyres and stars and has a 10" fitter. The clustered columnar standard is raised on a pedestal representing gothic architecture. It is unusual for the lower interior of the standard to be void. The entire standard rests on an octagonal stepped plinth. The surface is restored. Overall height: 35.5". $15,000-$20,000.

Detail of the burner label seen in previous lamp. It is inscribed: "Messenger & Sons 63 Hatton Garden London & Birmingham Manufactured for Alfred Welles Boston." Note that the name of Alfred Welles, the importer, is spelled out on a banner.

Pair of gilt lacquered brass and patinated bronze dual light Argand lamps, attributed to Messenger, second quarter nineteenth century. Swans are perched upon the urn shaped fonts. Tendrils and convolvuli stretch across the fuel feeder arms toward cut and etched blown glass shades with rolled rims. The double stepped plinth is raised on scrolled foliated feet. In original condition. Overall height: 18.5". $15,000-$18,000 for the pair.

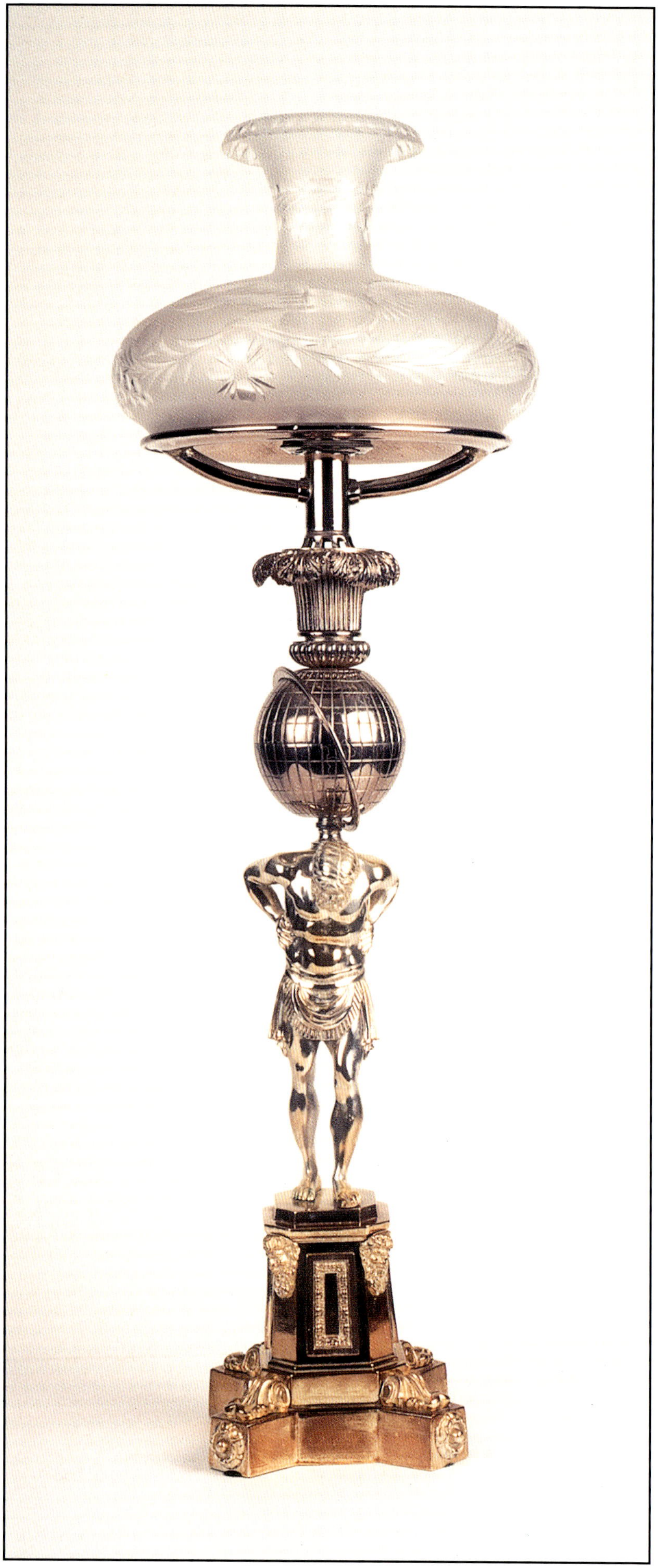

Signed electroplated silver sinumbra lamp, second quarter nineteenth century. The cast iron base weight in the plinth is stamped: "Messenger & Sons London." The 9" shade ring supports a cut and etched blown glass shade with rolled rim depicting doves carrying olive branches in their beaks. The foliated and reeded drip cup surmounts the heavens that Atlas supports upon his shoulders as he stands atop a pedestal. Masks, possibly the Four Winds, are applied to each corner of the pedestal. Scrolled leaves and lions' heads decorate the corners of the plinth. See pages 130, 139, 153, and 208 for lamps with similar bases and standards. The surface is restored. Height to the shade ring: 24.5". Overall height: 32". $18,000-$25,000.

Detail of dove designed globe seen in previous lamp.

Detail of the burner label seen in previous lamp.

Pair of patinated bronze dual light Argand lamps attributed to Messenger and Sons, second quarter nineteenth century. Labels attached to the burner tubes relate the name of the importer: "J & I Cox. New York." The cut and etched blown glass shades bear a fern and wheat motif. A bud finial is atop the reeded urn shaped font. Convolvuli and tendrils extend across the fuel feeder arms. Calices surmount an octagonal plinth adorned with applied masks and foliate decoration. Scrolled paw feet support the four corners of the base. In original condition. Overall height: 20.5". $12,000-$15,000 for the pair.

Signed pair of gilt lacquered brass and bronze sinumbra lamps, second quarter nineteenth century. The second brass casting from the bottom is signed: "Published As The Act Directs Messenger & Sons Birmingham." The reticulated trefoil shade rings have 9" diameter fitters and support cut and etched blown glass globes decorated with grape clusters and leaves. The winged Greek goddess of Victory, Nike, is personified in these standards. Hoisted above her head are the urn shaped drip cups bearing clusters of fruit. Nike stands atop a cylindrical pedestal decorated with applied festoons of flowers and grapes. An octagonal plinth with concave sides supports the entire standard. In original condition. Height to the shade ring: 26.5". Overall height: 35.5". $25,000-$30,000 for the pair.

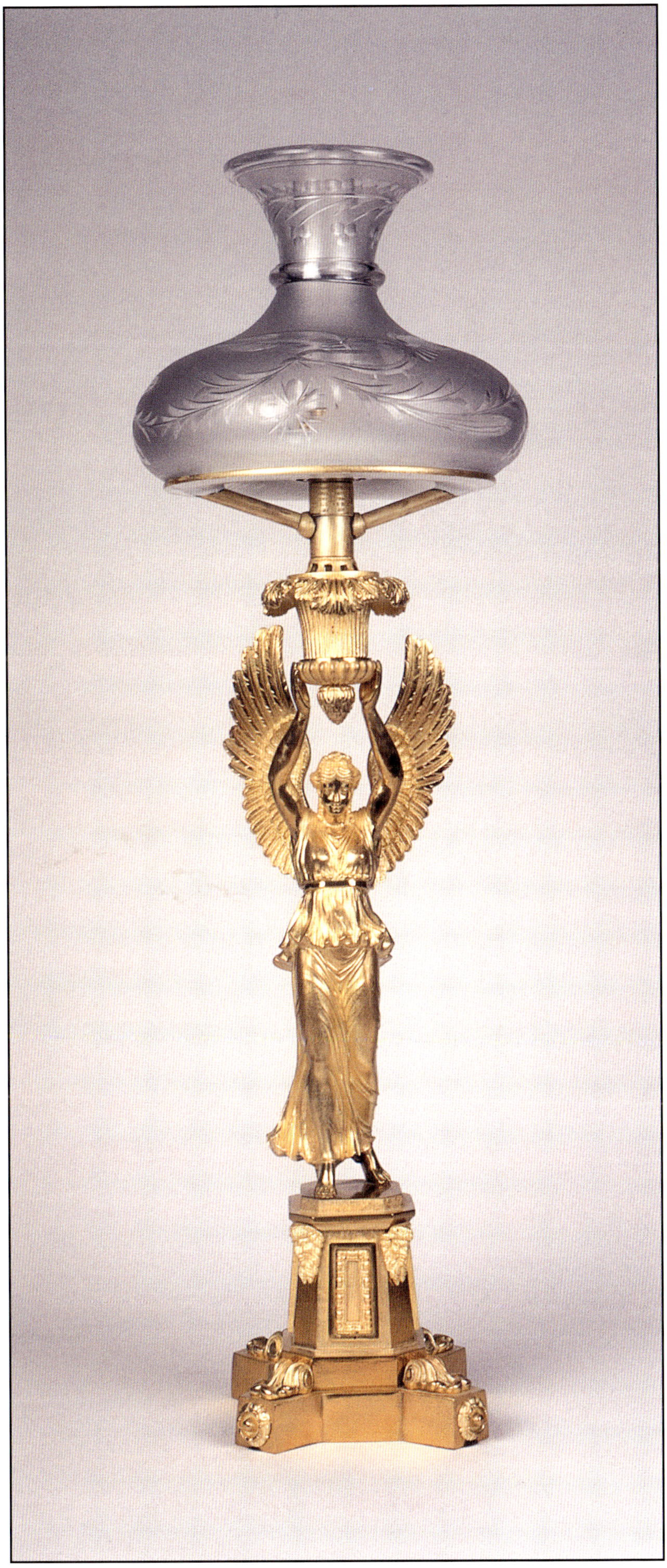

Signed gilt lacquered brass and bronze sinumbra lamp, second quarter nineteenth century. The cast iron base weight is stamped: "T C Salt." Salt, a well-known Birmingham, England lamp maker, is listed in the Wrightson's 1818 Directory of Birmingham as a: "lamp and lanthorn [lantern] manufacturer." The burner label reads: "Messenger & Sons London and Birmingham Manufactured for Jones, Lows & Ball Boston." The 8" diameter font holds a cut and etched blown glass shade ornamented with double doves and foliated decoration. The winged female figure, possibly Nike, hoists the urn shaped foliated drip cup above her head. She is poised atop an octagonal base and plinth that is adorned with applied masks, leaves and lions' faces. See lamps on pages 130, 136, 153, and 208 for similar bases/plinths. The surface is restored. Height to the shade ring: 24". Overall height: 32". $18,000-$22,000.

Detail of base seen in previous lamp.

Matching set of three patinated bronze Argand lamps, two single light and one dual light, attributed to Messenger, second quarter nineteenth century. A pair of dual light Argand lamps recently offered at the St. Charles Auction Gallery in New Orleans, Louisiana had identical bases and plinths to those pictured here. Brass plates affixed to the burner tubes of both of the auctioned lamps indicated that their manufacturer was Messenger and Sons. Urn shaped fonts with caryatid masks, are encircled by intimidating, twisted serpents. The gracefully curved, reeded fuel feeder arms are adorned by delicate convolvuli and spiraling tendrils. Three scrolled feet constitute the tripod base that is embellished with the faces of horned wolves. The shades are contemporary reproductions. Otherwise in original condition. Overall height: 20". $8,000-$10,000 for the set.

Detail of font seen in previous lamp.

Gilt lacquered brass and patinated bronze sinumbra lamp attributed to Messenger, second quarter nineteenth century. Retailer's label soldered to the burner tube reads: "J & I Cox New York." A border of palmettes surrounds the drip cup. Four tapered columns accented by applied foliated ormolu leaves comprise the standard. Petals, rosettes, leaves, and lilies ornament the base. Four neoclassical bearded masks, possibly the Four Winds, appear on each of the base's canted corners. Lions' paw feet resting on an accommodating plinth support the base and the standard. The cut and etched blown glass shade, with a 10" fitter, is decorated with geometric motifs and has a faceted neck and rim. In original condition. Height to the shade ring: 22.25". Overall height: 33.5". $15,000-$20,000.

Detail of faces seen in previous lamp.

Detail of base feet seen in previous lamp.

Detail of burner label seen in previous lamp.

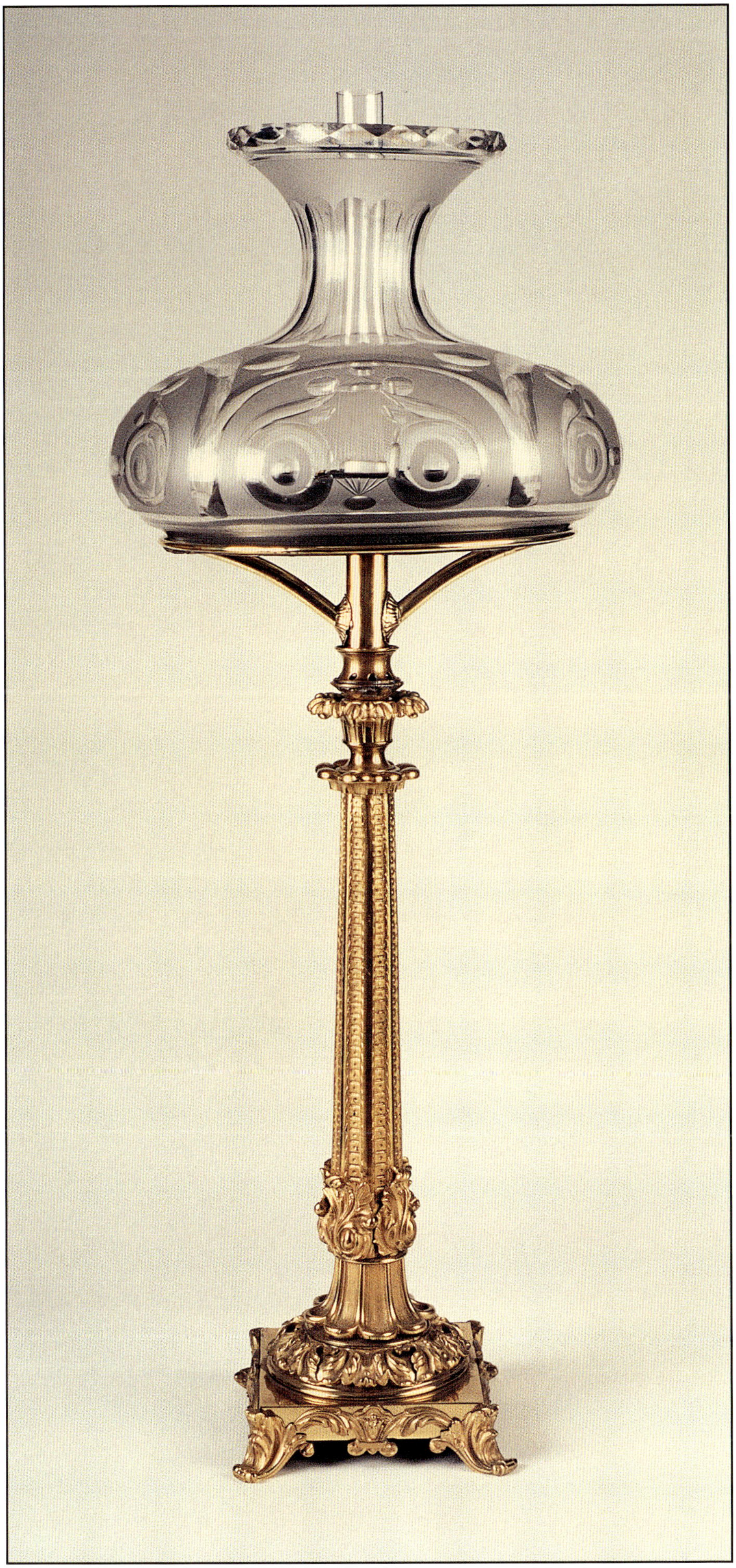

Graceful gilt lacquered brass and lacquered brass sinumbra lamp attributed to Messenger and Sons, second quarter nineteenth century. The 10" fitter diameter font supports an exquisite cut and etched blown glass shade depicting musical lyres. The neck and rim of the shade are faceted. A curved foliated drip cup surmounts a diaper patterned octagonal standard. Applied spiraling foliage envelops the base of the standard. Finely embossed leaves encircle the base. The square plinth is elevated on scroll feet. These identical feet have been seen on other lamps signed: "Messenger" (see pages 148 and 150). The surface is restored. Height to the shade ring: 23.5". Overall height: 33". $9,000-$12,000.

Detail of shade seen in previous lamp.

Illustration depicting original Messenger drawing of an urn whose shape was utilized in lamp castings. Written on the base of the urn is the name: "Messenger." Entitled: "Brough, Art Union January, 1846 p 6 18" high." *Courtesy: Birmingham Museum and Art Gallery.*

Opposite page: Two signed elaborate patinated bronze sinumbra lamps, second quarter nineteenth century. The second brass casting from the bottom bears the inscription: "Published As The Act Directs Messenger & Sons Birmingham." The fonts support cut and etched blown glass shades having 10" fitter diameters. Comprising the standards are graceful neoclassical maidens. Poised on their heads are drip cups in the form of urns filled with grape clusters and decorated with palmette leaves. The octagonal canted cornered plinths are decorated with scrolled modillions and palmette gadrooned edges. The surfaces are restored. Height to the shade rings: 25.5". Overall height: 33". $25,000-$30,000 for both.

Signed gilt lacquered brass and bronze sinumbra lamp, second quarter nineteenth century. A label affixed to the burner tube denotes the maker and the American importer: "Messenger & Sons London & Birmingham Manufactured for Jones, Lows & Ball Boston." The 10" fitter supports a cut and etched blown glass shade with dove and leaf designs. The upper half of the standard is reeded with applied palmettes. The lower half of the standard is composed of several different castings including an eagle, urn, and volutes with paw feet. The entire standard is raised on a circular plinth. The surface is restored. Height to the shade ring: 29.5". Overall height: 40". $18,000-$20,000.

Detail of eagle seen in previous lamp.

Detail of burner label seen in previous lamp.

Magnificent and intricate illustration entitled: "Metal Castings By Messenger and Sons." Handwritten into each corner are: "Birmingham" and "1849". This beautiful artwork embodies many of the classical features that made the company's lamps famous. Some of the distinctions include: Corinthian order, sarcophagus, putto, acanthi, griffins, and a maiden clad in a chiton. *Courtesy: Birmingham Museum and Art Gallery.*

Signed matching set of three lacquered brass and patinated bronze Argand lamps: two single light and one dual light, second quarter nineteenth century. The cast iron base weights of both single lamps are stamped: "Messenger." The dual light lamp does not have a manufacturer's mark although both burner tubes bear the brass retailer's plates marked: "B. Gardiner N. York." The abbreviated standard, base, feet, and glass shade designs are all identical to those shown on the accompanying sinumbra lamp by the same manufacturer and retailer (see page 150). The fuel reservoirs are in the form of fountains. Birds perched atop the pendant rings drink from the "fountains." The cut crystal pendants are of varying lengths simulating water overflowing the "fountains." The surfaces are restored. Overall height: 17". $15,000-$20,000 for the set.

Detail of base, plinth, and feet seen in previous lamps. Compare this to the sinumbra base, plinth, and feet seen on the accompanying sinumbra lamp, page 150.

Detail of burner label seen in previous lamps.

Detail of the fountain-like fuel reservoir and birds seen in the previous lamps. Note that the concept of a fountain and birds shown in the lower right corner of the illustration on page 147 has been applied to these castings.

N.YORK

Composite view of previously illustrated matching sinumbra and Argand lamps.

Opposite page;
Left: Signed gilt lacquered brass and patinated bronze sinumbra lamp, second quarter nineteenth century. The bottom of the cast iron base weight is stamped: "Messenger." The tapered standard decorated with a diaper design terminates into a foliated urn. The base is ornamented with embossed rosettes and cachepots containing floral bouquets. The squared triple plinth is supported on scrolled leaves. The burner tube exhibits the retail label of: "B Gardiner N York." The cut and etched blown glass shade has a 10" diameter fitter and is decorated in a repeating floral pattern accentuated with acorns. In original condition. Height to the shade ring: 22". Overall height: 31". $9,000-$10,000.

Top right: Detail of base, plinth, and feet seen in previous lamp.

Center right: Detail of cast iron base plate stamped: "Messenger" as seen in previous lamp.

Bottom right: Detail of burner label seen in previous lamp.

Signed gilt lacquered brass and bronze solar lamp, c. 1850. The cast iron base weight is stamped: "Messenger & Sons Published As The Act Directs." The bottom brass is signed: "Messenger." The 6" shade ring supports a ball form cut and etched blown glass globe with leaf designs. A likeness of Napoleon with the world and font balanced upon his head stands atop a cylindrical pedestal. Applied to the pedestal is a recumbent winged female figure lying atop a small mound of earth. The base and standard are raised on a square plinth. The surface is restored. Height to the shade ring: 22.5". Total height: 31". $10,000-$12,000.

Detail of the winged maiden seen in previous lamp. Allegorically, this figure may represent the fallen Nike, the Greek goddess of Victory, and reflect Napoleon's military and political demise. The inscription reads: "Isle D'Elbe." The French refer to Elba Island, as "Isle D'Elbe." This island is off the coast of Italy, where Napoleon lived in exile for eleven months during 1814-1815.

Pair of signed lacquered brass and patinated bronze rosin lamps, c. 1850. "Messenger & Sons London & Birmingham" is stamped into the cast iron base weights. Although the fonts have the inverted pear shape suggestive of solar lamps, the burners are designed to use rosin oil, presumably a mixture utilizing a hydrocarbon distillate. Ball form cut and etched blown glass globes are decorated in the "X and O" pattern. Coffin pendants are suspended from the 6" diameter shade rings. The standards are in the form of Atlas holding up the heavens on his shoulders. He is poised upon an octagonal base and an accommodating plinth with applied masks and scrolled leaves. See pages 130, 136, 139, and 208 for sinumbra lamps with similar standards and bases. In original condition. Height to the shade ring: 25". Overall height: 34". $15,000-$18,000 for the pair.

Gilt lacquered brass, lacquered brass, and bronze six light Argand chandelier attributed to Messenger and Sons, second quarter nineteenth century. The urn shaped font is decorated over its lower half with floral motifs. Radiating from the central dish are six fuel feeder tubes with applied leaves. Each burner supports a cut and etched blown glass shade decorated with leaves and berries and having a rolled rim. The base of the central dish is highly ornamented and terminates with a foliated finial. In original condition. Overall height: 24". $30,000-$35,000.

Opposite page: Detail of base seen in previous chandelier.

Beautiful foliated branches are illustrated in the form of a gasolier bracket or possibly for a chandelier arm. The handwriting denotes: "Messenger & Son made for competition for the Town hall art union January 1846 p 6." *Courtesy: Birmingham Museum and Art Gallery.*

Signed pair of gilt lacquered brass and bronze single light Argand style factory fitted spring loaded candle lamps, second quarter nineteenth century. Labels on the "burner tubes" read: "Messenger & Sons 20 Greville Street London & Birmingham." Three dolphins rest on the multiple tiered triangular plinths supporting the elongated reeded urn shaped "fonts," from which foliated bud finials and ornamented handles emerge. The burner arms emanate out from the "fonts" through the mouths of lions' masks. The cut and etched blown glass shades exhibit feather designs. Snowflake crystal pendants are suspended from the shade rings. In original condition. Height: 16.5". $12,500-$15,000 for the pair.

Detail of spring loaded candle mechanism seen in previous lamp.

Detail of "burner" label seen in previous lamp.

Classical and mythological motifs of acanthi, griffin, urns, amphorae, tripods, and standards are exhibited in this original illustration entitled: "Messenger & Son. Art Journal Janu-1846. p 6." The large urn in the upper left of the drawing is nearly identical to a Piranesi etching entitled: "Warwick Vase." *Courtesy: Birmingham Museum and Art Gallery.*

Chapter Five

The Cornelius Companies

The Philadelphia firm of Cornelius and Son was started in 1831 when Christian Cornelius, who had been a silversmith and lamp manufacturer for many years, was joined by his son, Robert. The firm directly competed with European imports that had dominated the lighting trade until the 1830s. In 1837, a city directory lists Cornelius and Son as lamp and chandelier makers working at 176 Chestnut Street.

In 1839, the firm's name changed to Cornelius and Company and remained as such until the death of Christian in 1851. At that time, Robert hired Christian's son-in-law, Isaac Baker, and the company became known as Cornelius and Baker. That year, the firm's fixtures were shown at the London Crystal Palace Exhibition. They were the only American company to exhibit lighting products there.

The firm became the largest manufacturer of lighting wares in North America. This advancement was due in part to Robert's business sense and technical knowledge. He received patents for improving the solar burner in 1843 and the solar wick raiser mechanism in 1849 (see below).

The Cornelius firms became known for high quality and large size castings. Early in their history, Cornelius produced Argand and sinumbra lamps. They were most famous for their ornate and efficient solar lamps that suited the taste of the wealthy. The Cornelius firm won several awards and its goods were sent to many foreign countries.

Two of Robert's sons joined the firm in 1861 and the name was changed to Cornelius, Baker and Company.

The following is a list of approximate dates and corresponding firm names:

1831-1839: Cornelius and Son
1839-1851: Cornelius and Company
1851-1861: Cornelius and Baker
1861-1870: Cornelius, Baker and Company
1870-1886: Cornelius and Sons
1886-1888: Cornelius and Hetherington
1888-1900: Cornelius and Rowland

Because of the firm's large size, it is likely that Cornelius supplied other lighting manufacturers and/or distributors with metal castings. Unfortunately, a catalogue prior to 1876 has not been found, but due to the company's large size and activity one almost certainly existed during the period 1831-1860. Letters addressed to Cornelius and Company, dated 1848 requesting descriptions and prices of four-light gas chandeliers with prysms (sic), suggest some type of drawing or catalogue may have been available at that time. We anxiously await the day when a catalogue will surface from some dusty attic in Philadelphia.

Argand and sinumbra lamps from Cornelius are often marked with the manufacturer's name on a brass plate soldered to the burner tube. Solar lamps have an elliptically shaped brass plate soldered to the font. This plate is usually stamped with the firm's name as well as patent date(s). These dates are April 1st, 1843 and July 24th, 1849.

The company's name has also been seen stamped on the cast iron base plate of Argand and sinumbra lamps as: "Cornelius," "Cornelius & Co," or "CC & Son."

Pair of gilt lacquered brass and bronze single light Argand lamps, second quarter nineteenth century (left and right). The standard is composed of a Roman centurion with one arm resting on his hip and the other on his sword while poised in a niche. The cast iron base weight contained within the plinth of the Argand lamps is stamped: "CC" probably for Christian Cornelius or Cornelius and Company. The 1850 Hooper catalogue illustrates a candelabra (item No. 318) showing a similar but not identical Roman centurion. Because of this somewhat conflicting information caution is urged in attributing these lamps to any one manufacturer. However, an authority on Philadelphia-manufactured Argand lamps assured the author that Cornelius produced these lamps. They are in original condition. Height to the font finial: 25". In the center is an unmarked gilt lacquered brass and bronze sinumbra lamp, second quarter nineteenth century, attributed to Cornelius. The standard is in the form of a vase fuseau raised above a pedestal displaying a Roman centurion identical to those found on the Argand lamps. The surface finish has been restored. Overall height: 31". It is interesting to note that all three cut and etched blown glass shades are of a conforming design. $25,000-$35,000 for the set of three.

Opposite page, left: Gilt lacquered brass and lacquered brass signed Cornelius and Company solar lamp, c. 1850. The font retains its original burner components and supports a cut and etched blown glass globe with faceted neck ornamented by an American shield and having a 5" wide fitter. The fluted standard is raised on a double marble plinth. The shade ring supports spear-point crystal pendants. Height to the shade ring: 13.25" Overall height: 23.25". $2,500-$3,000.

Detail of the American shield seen on the globe in previous lamp.

Labeled Cornelius and Baker gilt lacquered bronze, patinated bronze, and brass solar lamp, c. 1851. The lamp contains its original burner mechanism and supports a finely cut and etched blown glass globe that displays a Federal shield and has a 6" diameter fitter. The standard is possibly of English origin. Colonial pendants are suspended from the shade ring. In original condition. Height to the shade ring: 19.5". Overall height: 28". $2,800-$3,500.

Labeled gilt lacquered brass and brass hanging solar lamp, c.1845. The label soldered to the font is inscribed: "Cornelius & Co. Patent Philad. April 1st, 1843." The font is suspended from the foliated corona by circular and rectangular links of chain. Entwined serpents connect the suspension chains to the font's brackets. The 5" fitter supports a shade from a later period. Otherwise in original condition. Overall height: 29". $2,500-$3,500.

Detail of label seen on lamp at right.

Unusual labeled Cornelius and Baker solar lamp, c. 1851. The lamp is composed of patinated spelter, gilt lacquered brass, and patinated brass. The standard is in the form of three conjoined female figures on a single marble base. The font is equipped with a factory fitted burner that supports a cut and etched blown glass "Oregon" style shade with a 3" diameter fitter (top mount). Height to the shade ring: 14". Overall height: 24.5". $1,800-$2,200.

Labeled Cornelius and Baker gilt lacquered bronze and brass solar lamp, c. 1851. The font retains its original burner mechanism and supports a turban form cut and etched blown glass shade with a 6" wide fitter. The finely cast standard is in the form of a classical maiden, one hand raised above her head, the other resting on her hip. A lamp with a nearly identical standard appears in the Dietz catalogue on Plate 32, item No. 149. The lamp is supported by a double marble plinth. Height to the shade ring: 15.75". Overall height: 27.75". $2,800-$3,500.

Labeled Cornelius and Company gilt lacquered brass and bronze solar lamp, c.1850. The stenciled standard rests on a double marble plinth. The font has a factory fitted burner. The cut and etched blown glass globe is decorated with gothic windows and has a 6" diameter fitter. Height to the shade ring: 12.75". Overall height: 22.5". $3,000-$3,500.

Labeled Cornelius and Company gilt lacquered brass and bronze solar lamp, c. 1850. The font has an original burner. The finely cut and etched blown glass globe is double waisted with a rolled rim and a 6" diameter fitter. The bulbous standard is raised on a spreading plinth resting on scroll feet. 7" back-cut Albert pendants are suspended from the shade ring. Height to the shade ring: 14". Overall height: 27". $4,000-$5,000.

Signed gilt lacquered brass and lacquered brass hanging camphene burning hall lantern fitted with a six-spout burner, second quarter nineteenth century. Affixed to the font is an elliptically shaped brass plate inscribed: "Cornelius & Co. Philadelphia." Suspended from the delicately embossed shade ring encircling the font are back-cut Albert pendants. The cut etched and blown glass globe is decorated with vines and flowers. The reticulated shade bezel is composed of scrolls and contains three foliated brackets from which suspension chains attach to the corona. In original condition. Overall height: 35". $18,000-$22,000.

Labeled Cornelius and Baker gilt lacquered brass and brass solar lamp, c.1851. The font is fitted with a factory burner mechanism. The cut and etched blown glass "Oregon" style shade has a 6" diameter fitter. Grotesque masks ornament the foliated triangular standard. Height to the shade ring: 13.75". Overall height: 27.5". $1,800-$2,200.

Labeled Cornelius and Baker patinated spelter and brass camphene lamp, c. 1851. The four prong burner retains all of its original extinguisher caps. The standard is in the form of three conjoined female figures raised on a square marble plinth. Height to the shade ring: 13.75". Overall height: 21.5". $1,800-$2,200.

Labeled Cornelius brass solar lamp, c. 1845. An elliptical metal plate soldered to the font reads: "Cornelius & Co. Philad. Patent April 1st. 1843." The cut and etched blown glass shade has a 5" diameter fitter. Snowflake pendants hang from the shade ring. A reeded standard terminating into an ornate cast Corinthian capital supports the font. The square plinth is accented with rosettes and cabochons set in cartouches. The surface is restored. Height to the shade ring: 16.5". Overall height: 26.5". $2,000-$2,500.

Opposite page, bottom right: Labeled Cornelius and Baker gilt lacquered brass and bronze solar lamp, c. 1851. The font has a factory burner mechanism and supports a double waisted cut and etched blown glass shade with a rolled rim and a 6" diameter fitter. The standard is modeled in the Rococo Revival style and rests on a stellate plinth. Original finish. Overall height: 27". $4,500-$5,500.

Labeled Cornelius and Baker gilt lacquered brass and bronze solar lamp, c. 1851. The bulbous standard is raised on a stepped marble plinth. The font contains an original burner and displays a rare turban form cut and etched blown glass shade with a 6.5" diameter fitter. Height to the shade ring: 13.75". Overall height: 26.25". $2,200-$2,800.

Labeled Cornelius and Baker gilt lacquered bronze, brass, and spelter solar lamp, c. 1851. The font retains its original burner mechanism. The double waisted cut and etched blown glass globe is decorated with geometric designs, has a faceted neck, rolled rim, and a 6" wide fitter. The standard is in the form of a classical maiden. The figure is gilded spelter and is raised on a double marble plinth. Height to the shade ring: 16.75". Overall height: 29.75". $5,000-$6,000.

Labeled Cornelius and Company tin and brass solar lamp, c. 1850. This lamp was probably designed for commercial use. The font has its factory fitted burner components. The burner supports a top mount cut and etched ball form blown glass shade with a 3" fitter diameter. Height to the shade ring: 11". Overall height: 21". $500-$800.

Labeled Cornelius and Baker tin solar lamp, c.1851. The font retains its original burner that supports a top mount cut and etched spherical blown glass shade having a 3" wide fitter. This model is also produced in brass. Height to the top of the font: 11.75". Overall height: 22.25". $500-$1,000.

Labeled Cornelius and Baker gilt lacquered brass and brass solar lamp, c. 1851. The font contains the factory equipped burner and supports a 5" fitter diameter cut and etched blown glass shade. The standard is in the form of a foliated tripod. The surface is partially restored. Height to the shade ring: 13". Overall height: 26". $1,800-$2,200.

Labeled Cornelius and Baker gilt lacquered brass and bronze solar lamp, c. 1851. The triangular standard rests on scroll feet. The font contains a solar burner and supports a bulbous cut and etched blown glass shade decorated with geometric motifs. The shade has a faceted neck, rolled rim, and a 5" diameter fitter. Height to the shade ring: 13.5". Overall height: 21.25". $1,800-$2,200.

Signed gimbaled gilt lacquered brass spring loaded candle lamp, c. 1851. A label affixed to the standard reads: "Cornelius & Baker Philadelphia." In original condition. Overall height: 14". $1,500-$1,800.

Labeled Cornelius and Baker tin utilitarian carrying solar lamp and wall sconce, c. 1851. The font retains the original factory burner. The light is intensified with the use of a circular concave reflector with central convexity. Overall height: 13". $600-$900.

Unusual gilt lacquered bronze timepiece holder attributed to Cornelius and Company. The standard is referred to as the "bear and beehive" and is incorporated in girandoles produced by various manufacturers. Overall height: 15". $600-$800.

Chapter Six

William Carleton

William Carleton was born in Haverhill, Massachusetts, educated in the public school system, and did not attend college. As other family members had done before him, Carleton served an apprenticeship to a copper and tinsmith completing his training at age twenty-one.

C. 1850 portrait of William Carleton (May 20, 1797-December 5, 1876). *Courtesy of the Archives Department, Carleton College.*

Silk ribbon advertising Carleton's brass works presented on September 17, 1856. *Courtesy of the Archives Department, Carleton College.*

In 1818, Carleton moved to Charlestown, Massachusetts, where he was temporarily employed as a metal worker on Main Street.

Shortly thereafter, he relocated to Boston where he first appears in the city directory of 1820 as a "tinman" located at 9 Marlboro Street.

Over the next several years, Carleton's business had different Boston addresses, including Harvard Place, a tiny recess off Washington Street near the Old South Meeting House. During this time, although remaining a "tinman" in the directories, he secured a patent for a gas light fixture that became quite successful. As his trade expanded, the production of lighting devices became his sole business. The company was first listed as a "lamp manufacturer" in the 1841 city directory.

In 1834, the firm's rapid expansion necessitated a move to a larger facility located at 12 Beach Street in Boston. Carleton's business remained at this location for the next fifty years. He was thought to be the first man of Boston to use a stationary steam engine to run his machinery.

The company grew to become one of the nation's larger manufacturers of lamps and gas fixtures. As his business flourished, Carleton became active in associated endeavors. At different times he was organizer, director, and president of the Charlestown Gas Company. Carleton also became a director of the New England and Boston and Sandwich Glass Companies.

Between 1837 and 1863, Carleton's personal residence was 16 Harvard Street in the Charlestown neighborhood of Boston. His next home was a townhouse on Monument Square that he designed.

Carleton's townhouse on Monument Square in Boston, where he lived from 1863 until his death in 1876 (photograph c. 1990). *Courtesy of the Archives Department, Carleton College.*

The Edward Everett House, Carleton's home in the Charlestown area of Boston from 1837-1863 (photograph c. 1990). *Courtesy of the Archives Department, Carleton College.*

With the advent of kerosene, the firm was able to make the transition to this type of fuel. In 1869, Carleton and Rufus S. Merrill secured a patent relating to the external sleeve on the wick tube of a kerosene burner.

In 1871, Carleton became the $50,000 benefactor to the Northfield, Minnesota college that bears his name today. In today's money, this donation would be the equivalent of approximately $4,000,000.

It is unclear how consistently Carleton lighting wares display the manufacturer's mark. The few marked sinumbra and solar lamps that we have seen bear a brass plate soldered to the burner tube and inscribed: "Manufactured by W. Carleton Boston." The cast iron base plate in the Argand lamp illustrated in this text is stamped: "WC".

Labeled W. Carleton gilt and patinated bronze sinumbra lamp, second quarter nineteenth century. The font supports a cut and etched blown glass shade that has an 8" diameter fitter and is decorated with classical lyres and stars. The shade neck is faceted, as is the rim. The standard is in the form of an angel. The pedestal displays, in relief, a youthful Hercules carrying a slain lion and boar. Leaves border the square stepped plinth. In original condition. Overall height: 32". $15,000-$20,000.

Detail of the burner label seen in the previous lamp, reading: "Manufactured W. Carleton Boston."

Detail of the pedestal seen in the previous lamp.

Detail of the shade seen in the previous lamp.

Labeled diminutive W. Carleton patinated bronze sinumbra lamp, second quarter nineteenth century. This lamp is often referred to as a "miniature" sinumbra. The cut and etched blown glass shade has a 5 3/8" diameter fitter and is raised above a columnar standard resting on a square plinth. The burner label reads: "Manufactured by W. Carleton Boston." In original condition. Overall height: 17". $3,500-$5,500.

Labeled W. Carleton patinated bronze sinumbra lamp, second quarter nineteenth century. The 8" fitter diameter etched and cut blown glass shade is decorated with arches, diamonds, and foliage. A fluted pedestal joined by dolphins and resting on a shaped plinth supports the standard, which is in the form of a standing maiden with arms raised. The burner label reads: "Manufactured by W Carleton Boston." In original condition. Height to the shade ring: 20.25". Overall height: 27.75". $12,000-$16,000.

Signed W. Carleton dual light lacquered brass and patinated bronze Argand lamp, second quarter nineteenth century. The cast iron base weight in the plinth is stamped: "WC." The urn shaped fuel reservoir is decorated with a foliate finial, vines, and Georgian crystal pendants. The standard is in the form of an eagle with spread wings. The beaded base exhibits grotesque masks and rests on a square plinth raised by winged paw feet. Georgian crystal pendants are also suspended from rings on the burner tubes separate from the shade rings (see Figure 7, page 16). The etched and cut blown glass trumpet style shades have geometric designs and faceted rims. The surface is restored. Overall height: 23.5". $6,000-$8,000.

Detail of eagle seen in the previous lamp.

Detail of the globe seen in the previous lamp.

Detail of the base, plinth, and feet seen in the previous lamp.

Detail of the cast iron base plate stamped with the initials "WC" seen in the previous lamp.

Labeled miniature gilt brass sinumbra lamp, second quarter nineteenth century. A label affixed to the burner tube is embossed: "Manufactured by W Carleton Boston." The 5.375" fitter diameter cut and etched blown glass shade is decorated with geometric designs and has a faceted rim and neck. Balancing an entablature atop her head with her outstretched arms, the classical caryatid is poised on a cylindrical marble pedestal that rests upon a square marble plinth. In original condition. Height to the shade ring: 11". Overall height: 17". $5,000-$6,000.

Detail of burner label seen on the previous lamp.

Unusual signed W. Carleton tin, patinated, and gilt bronze Argand wall sconce, which may also be used as a table lamp. Trefoils border the mirrored reflector. The burner label reads: "Manufactured by W Carleton Boston." In original condition. Overall height: 10". $1,000-$1,500.

Chapter Seven

Other Lesser Known & Unknown Manufacturers

Much like a fireworks show, in some respects the best lighting examples have been saved for last. As you flip though these pages, you will see some of the largest, most ornate, and aesthetically pleasing Argand, sinumbra, and solar lighting devices. The use of figural standards, mythology characters, and animals abound.

It is unclear why many manufactures did not consistently mark their lighting wares. The author has personally disassembled Argand and sinumbra lamps that appear to be the work of Messenger only to find all castings devoid of a manufacturer's mark. For this reason, great care and thought should be used before attributing a particular lamp to a specific maker.

Furthermore, it is generally believed that identical metal castings made by one company were often sold to or pirated by another firm that perhaps did not have a foundry. Therefore, just because a casting looks like it was made by Messenger doesn't necessarily mean that it comprises a Messenger lamp. In addition, castings from several different manufacturers are interchangeable.

The author has attempted to be objective and conservative in categorizing lighting devices as having an unknown or known manufacturer. Certainly many of the lamps illustrated on the following pages were made by well-known manufacturers that simply did not mark the piece or placed their mark on a part of the lamp that is no longer present (i.e., deflector on Hooper solar burners).

Opposite page: A plate from an unknown English lamp manufacturer's pattern book, c. 1825, depicting three sinumbra lamps with different heights, standards, and shade fitter diameters. Some lighting experts have questioned the production of sinumbra lamps with figural standards. The example on the far right illustrates that such lamps existed at least in pattern books and the numerous illustrations in this text document that they were readily available to those customers so inclined. Interchangeable metal castings would make the existence of figural sinumbra lamps intuitively obvious (also see the Hooper catalogue illustrations, page 62). Note the top caption that reads "Glasses are charged separately," indicating that the lamp prices do not include the shade and chimney. Observe the prices and see that the figural lamp, while not the largest, is the most expensive. The price quotations are in the archaic method of denoting shillings in which 20 shillings were equal to £1; therefore, 50/- shillings equals £2.50.
Left: #585, height of standard: 16" with a 9" diameter fitter, 32/- shillings each
Middle: #582, height of standard: 23" with a 10" diameter fitter, 50/- shillings each
Right: #642, height of standard: 18" with a 9" diameter fitter, 52/- shillings each
Courtesy: Victoria and Albert Museum.

Glasses are charged Separately
9 In.
16 In.
585 32/- Ea
10 In.
23 In.
582 50/- Ea
9 In.
18 In.
642 52/- Ea

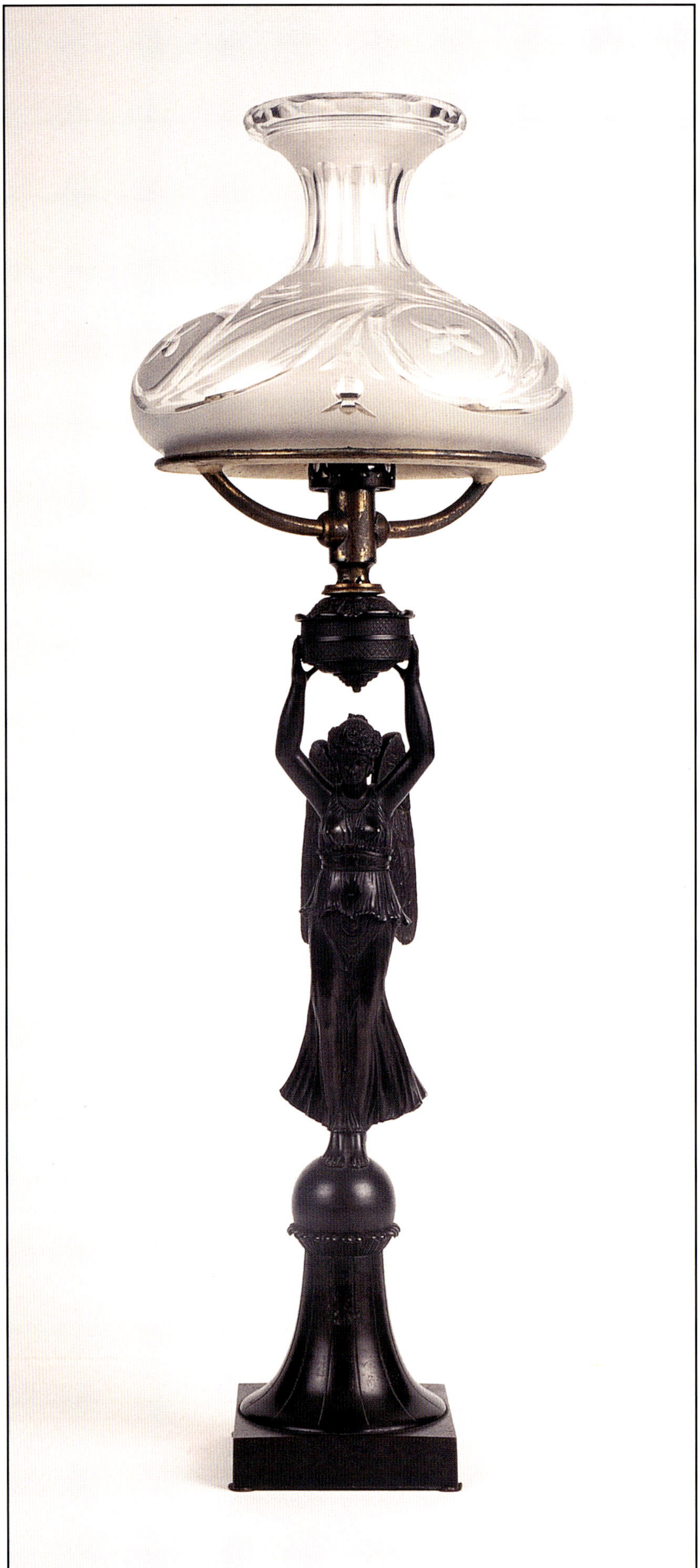

Patinated brass and bronze sinumbra lamp, English or American, second quarter nineteenth century. The cut and etched blown glass shade with a 9" fitter rests on a ring form fuel reservoir. The burner sits in a roundel held aloft by the figure of Winged Victory, the goddess Nike, standing on an orb. The tapered pedestal is raised on a square plinth. In original condition. Overall height: 33". $18,000-$22,000.

English or American gilt lacquered and patinated brass and bronze solar lamp, c. 1850. The standard is in the form of Winged Victory, yet another artist's rendition of the Greek goddess Nike, her hands raised above her head. The font is equipped with its original burner elements. The cut and etched blown glass globe has a 6" diameter fitter and is decorated with geometric designs. The globe has an everted neck and a rolled rim. Albert pendants adorn the shade ring. In original condition. Height to the shade ring: 20.25". Overall height: 31". $6,000-$9,000.

Impressive and stately dual light patinated bronze Argand lamp, maker unknown but probably English, second quarter nineteenth century. A sprouting bud emerges from the urn shaped scroll handled font. Highly ornamental arabesque branches compose the fuel feeder arms that terminate into acanthi embossed burner tubes and drip cups. Elaborately cut and etched blown glass shades with faceted necks rest upon the reticulated shade rings. Hercules, with serpents entwined around his wrists, supports a reeded cauldron upon his back. He wears a bearskin as a helmet with the bear's face on top of his head. The round plinth supports a grape and acanthi embellished base. In original condition. Overall height: 32.5". $25,000-$30,000.

Lacquered brass hanging solar lamp, manufacturer unknown, c. 1850. The font contains a 3/4" burner. The etched and cut blown glass shade exhibits floral designs, a faceted neck, and rolled rim. Three chains and brackets suspend the font under the smoke bell. In original condition. Overall height: 18". $3,000-$4,000.

Detail of Hercules's face seen in the previous lamp.

Pair of gilt lacquered brass and patinated bronze single light Argand lamps in the Egyptian Revival Style, manufacturer unknown, possibly Bullock, c. 1825. The cut etched and blown glass shades are decorated with floral motifs. A flame finial emerges from the urn shaped fonts that are decorated with applied gilded wreaths. Acanthi encircle the standards. The handles are in the likeness of coiled serpents. Neoclassical female masks are applied to the sides of the lamps. Paw feet, scrolled leaves, and rosettes support the circular plinths. The surfaces have been restored. Overall height: 13.5". $18,000-$20,000 for the pair.

Opposite page: Pair of gilt lacquered brass solar lamps, manufacturer unknown, c. 1850. The fonts contain 9/16" burners. Ball form cut and etched blown glass shades set atop 4" fitter diameter shade rings. The standards are in the form of spread wing eagles adorned with laurel wreaths around their necks. The eagles are poised atop reeded columns above an embossed socle. The surfaces are restored. Height to the shade ring: 13". Overall height: 18.5". $7,500-$10,000 for the pair.

Pair of Sheffield silver dual light Argand lamps, c. 1815. Manufacturer unknown but probably English. These are the earliest Argand lamps illustrated in this book. Urn shaped fonts sit atop cylindrical standards and plinths. The shades are wonderfully cut and etched blown glass decorated with spread wing eagles majestically perched atop American shields. Inscribed into the rippling banners on the shades is the Latin phrase: *E Pluribus Unum* ("Out of Many One"). In original condition. Height from the plinth to the font finial: 20". $20,000-$25,000 for the pair.

Detail of globe seen in previous lamps.

Gilt lacquered brass and bronze and cut crystal solar lamp, c. 1850, maker unknown. The rare turban form cut and etched blown glass shade with a 6" fitter is decorated in the "Diamond and Thousand Eye" pattern. The font contains a 3/4" burner. The bulbous glass standard is raised on a circular plinth. The cut glass dish below the font would have supported glass pendants (now missing). Otherwise in original condition. Height to the shade ring: 13.75". Overall height: 24". $4,500-$5,500.

Gilt lacquered brass and lacquered brass four light solar chandelier, c. 1850. All fonts are signed: "Archer & Warner Philadelphia." The reeded shaft descends from the foliated and grape clustered corona to the central dish in which three graceful neoclassical maidens are poised. Delicate chains of pierced anthemia connect the corona to the scrolled branching arms. Albert pendants are suspended from the font rings. The cut and etched blown glass shades exhibit geometric motifs. In original condition. Overall height: 40". $25,000-$30,000.

Detail of the maidens seen in the previous chandelier.

Gilt lacquered brass and bronze sinumbra lamp, second quarter nineteenth century, bearing the retailer's label of: "Stoutenburgh & Cox New York" on the burner tube. The cut and etched blown glass shade has a faceted everted rim, narrow neck, and 10" diameter fitter; the waist displays foliate motifs. The columnar standard is interrupted by leaves and is raised above a spreading socle and a square plinth. In original condition. Overall height: 32.5". $10,000-$12,000.

Detail of burner label seen in previous lamp.

Pair of patinated bronze dual light Argand lamps, second quarter nineteenth century. All four burner plates bear the retailer's label and are embossed: "Clark Coit & Cargill N. York." The shade rings support cut and etched floral designed blown glass globes with rolled rims. Since rotation of the shade ring raises and lowers the wick, pendants cannot be hung directly on this device or they would abut the fuel feeder arm with each rotation. Therefore, directly below the shade rings are additional rings from which uniform length Georgian pendants hang. This is an important distinction. If one finds an Argand lamp with pendants attached directly to the shade ring they are clearly a later addition when the spiral wick raiser mechanism was no longer needed, i.e. the lamp has been converted to burn kerosene or electrified (see Figure 7, page 16). Buds emanate from the reeded fonts. Georgian pendants of varying lengths that simulate cascading water are suspended from reticulated font rings. Volutes and convolvuli adorn the fuel feeder arms and the tripod plinths. In original condition. Overall height: 17". $18,000-$20,000 for the pair.

American or English gilt lacquered, patinated bronze, and brass sinumbra lamp, second quarter nineteenth century, manufacturer unknown. The cut and etched blown glass shade, with an unusual 7.5" diameter fitter, rests on a circular font decorated with a repoussé brass border. The columnar standard is raised atop a fluted pedestal resting on a square plinth. The surface is restored. Overall height: 22.5". $8,000-$10,000.

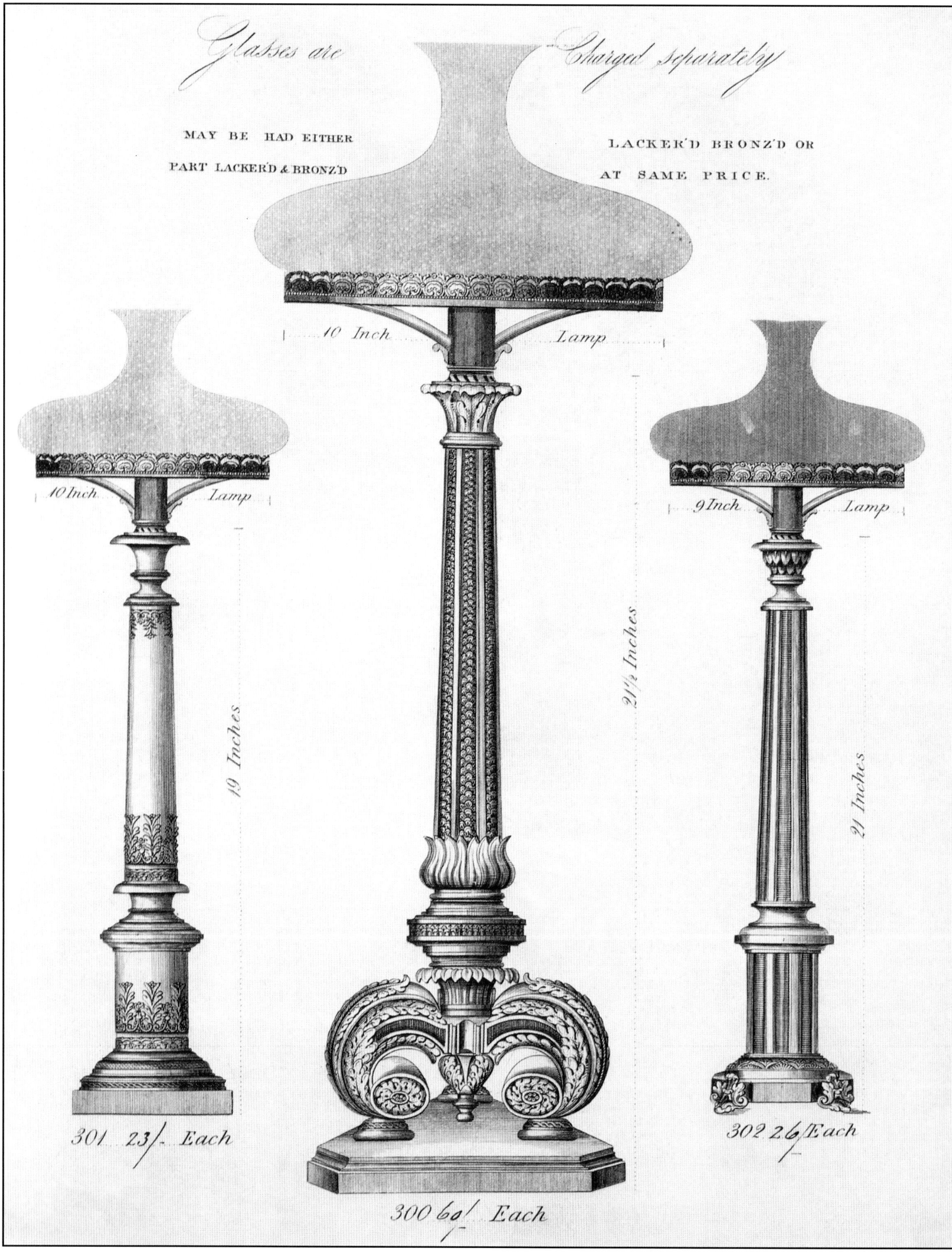
Glasses are Charged separately
MAY BE HAD EITHER
PART LACKER'D & BRONZ'D
LACKER'D BRONZ'D OR
AT SAME PRICE.
10 Inch Lamp
10 Inch Lamp
9 Inch Lamp
19 Inches
21½ Inches
21 Inches
301 23/- Each
300 60/- Each
302 26/- Each

Gilt lacquered brass, lacquered brass, and patinated bronze three light Argand chandelier, manufacturer unknown, second quarter nineteenth century. A flame finial sits atop a vasiform font that is circumferentially surrounded by applied leaves and acorns. Connecting the corona to the foliated twisted brackets are suspension chains composed of alternating round and ovoid links. The cut and etched and blown glass globes are decorated with leaves and berries. In original condition. Overall height: 21". $20,000-$25,000.

Opposite page: A plate from an unknown English lamp manufacturer's pattern book depicting three sinumbra lamps, c.1825. The glass shades were sold separately. Each price is written in the archaic method of denoting shillings (see page 181).
Left: #301, height of the standard: 19" tall with a 10" fitter diameter, 23/- each
Middle: #300, height of the standard: 21.25" tall with a 10" fitter diameter, 60/- each
Right: #307, height of the standard: 24" tall with a 9" fitter diameter, 26/- each
Courtesy: Victoria and Albert Museum.

Opposite page: Pair of American or English gilt lacquered and patinated bronze and brass stand Argand lamps, first quarter nineteenth century. The cut and etched blown glass shades are seated with a set screw. The urn shaped fonts are raised on foliated pedestals. The stepped plinth is bordered by leaves and raised on toupie feet. In original condition. Overall height: 19". $2,500-$3,000.

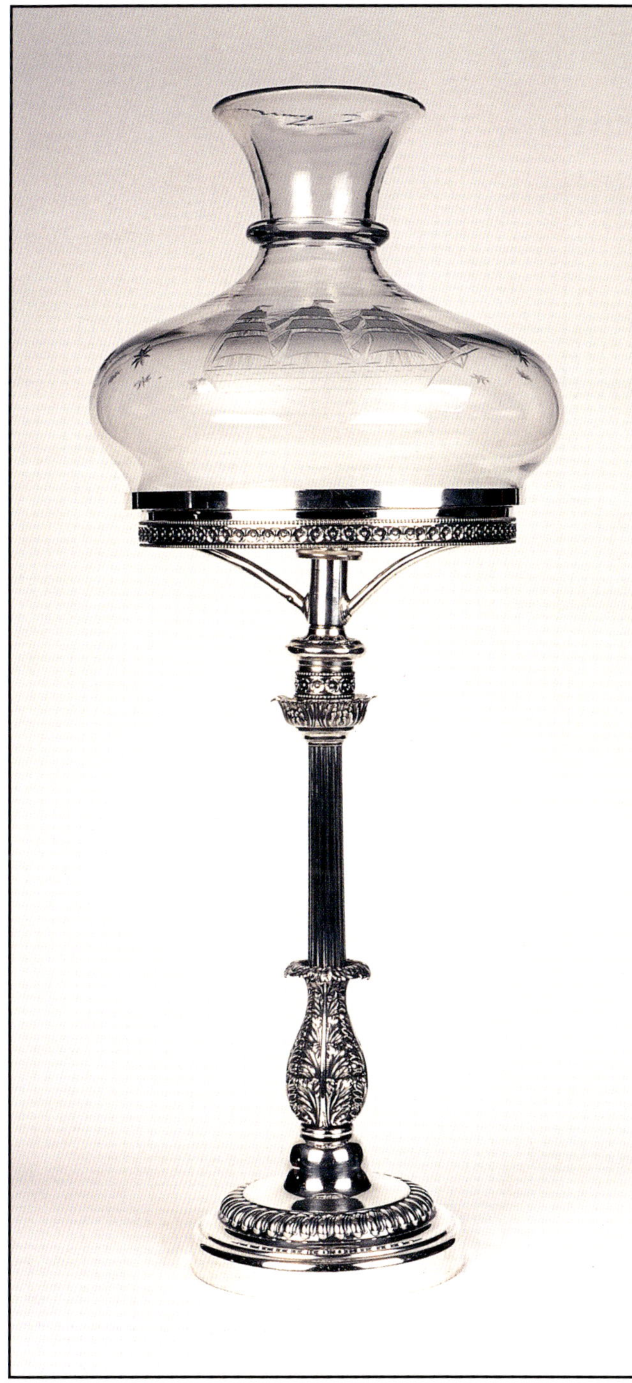

Sheffield silver sinumbra lamp, manufacturer unknown, first quarter nineteenth century. The unusually large 11" embossed shade ring holds a gracefully cut and etched blown glass globe decorated with a three-masted schooner and twelve stars. The reeded standard emerges from a foliated vase. Gadrooned edges encircle the round plinth. The surface is restored. Height to the shade ring: 22". Overall height: 34". $28,000-$32,000.

Detail of the globe seen in the previous lamp.

Extraordinary pair of gilt lacquered brass and lacquered brass single light Argand lamps in their original selling cases, manufacturer unknown, second quarter nineteenth century. These lamps are considered "New Old Stock," i.e., never having been used before. Urn shaped fonts are decorated with a crown of curved petals. Large scrolled acanthi support the burners on which rest the cut and etched blown glass globes. The design cut on the interior of the rim of the globes matches the crown of petals on the font. The square plinth rests on scrolled foliated feet. In original condition. Overall height: 20.25" $25,000-$30,000 for the pair.

Detail of the lamps at right seen without their glass case covers.

Detail of interior globe rim and font crown seen in the lamps above right.

Patinated bronze watch stand, manufacturer unknown, possibly English, second quarter nineteenth century. A classical running maiden atop a cylindrical base comprises the standard. In her raised left hand she holds a hook from which a pocket watch is suspended. This hook, in actuality, is a fuel valve adjustment lever for an Argand lamp (see Figure 9, page 17). Once again this illustrates the utilization of castings for different purposes. In original condition. $2,500-$3,000.

Detail of hook (fuel valve adjustment lever) seen in the previous watch stand.

Gilt lacquered brass and patinated bronze three light Argand chandelier, manufacturer unknown, second quarter nineteenth century. The upper canopy is adorned with large rosettes and leaves. The urn shaped font displays a crown of palmettes and a bud finial. Applied rosettes, foliage, cabochons, and berries decorate the sides of the font. Highly ornamented links comprise the suspension chains. Acanthi leaves garnish the patinated base. Cut and etched blown glass globes with floral designs and rolled rims rest atop the burners. In original condition. Overall height: 28". $20,000-$25,000.

Hanging Argand lamp of unlacquered brass, manufacturer unknown, second quarter nineteenth century. Lamps similar but not identical to this one are illustrated in the 1850 Hooper catalogue as item No. 498; in the 1860 Dietz catalogue, on Plate 31, item No. 19; and in the Starr, Fellows 1856 catalogue in the section entitled: "Hanging Oil Lamps." The font sits in a ring to which delicate foliage and coiled tendrils attach, constituting the support brackets for the suspension chains. This lamp is pictured with a reproduction solar chimney. The burner is missing its flame deflector hence the term Argand. Installation of the flame deflector would convert this to a solar burner and change the name of the lamp to a hanging solar. Therefore, as mentioned in the Overview and elsewhere, it is not the configuration of the font but the type of burner that determines the proper terminology for a lighting device. In original condition. Overall length: 19". $3,000-$4,000.

On the left, an unusual patinated pewter solar lamp, manufacturer unknown, c. 1850. The font retains its factory installed burner components. The baluster standard rests on a socle. In original condition. Overall height: 15.50". $800-$1,200. On the right is a rare American gilt lacquered brass and bronze solar lamp having a molded glass font signed: "R. A. Spalding." The pedestal is in the form of a candle cup raised on a spreading socle and square marble plinth. In original condition. Overall height: 18". $800-$1,200.

Unusual hand-held gilt lacquered brass and lacquered brass solar lamp. Set screws hold the bulbous "Oregon" style cut and etched blown glass shade with a 2.5" fitter. A loop handle joins the urn form font. The breather is integrated to the circular plinth. The surface is restored. Overall height: 10". $500-$900.

Gilt lacquered brass and brass camphene burning lamp, manufacturer unknown. The cut and etched blown glass shade is raised above the font and rests on a 5" wide fitter. The four prong burner mechanism retains its original extinguisher caps. The bulbous standard displays a cameo of George Washington and rests on a double marble base. This lamp is illustrated in the *Smithsonian Bulletin* No. 141 on Plate 62. In original condition. Overall height: 25.5". $1,800-$2,200.

Gilt lacquered brass and bronze lithophane stand. The "Iris" pattern standard is seen in the catalogues of several different lighting manufacturers. The frame now contains a photographic image on white glass. This is one more example of a lamp standard casting used for products other than lamps. In original condition. Overall height: 22". $400-$700.

Detail of burner and wick raiser mechanism seen in previous lamp.

Tin and brass hanging sinumbra lamp, manufacturer unknown, first quarter nineteenth century. The cut and etched blown glass shade demonstrates gothic spire designs and has a 10" diameter fitter. The shade rests on a green painted font that is suspended by three brass rods attached to a foliated corona. The wick raiser functions by the rack and pinion mechanism. In original condition. Overall length: 60". $10,000-$11,000.

Pair of dual light crystal, gilt lacquered brass, lacquered brass, and patinated bronze Argand lamps, manufacturer unknown, second quarter nineteenth century. Volutes spread across the fuel feeder arms. Diamond-cut, diaper-designed crystal envelops the central standard rods and glass fonts. The cut and etched blown glass globes exhibit the same diamond-cut diaper design. The base is composed of four crystal columns that sit atop a multi-tiered circular brass plinth; together these replicate a neoclassical garden temple. In original condition. Overall height: 30.5". $28,000-$32,000 for the pair.

Pair of gilt lacquered and patinated bronze stenciled whale oil lamps presented to an otherwise unknown individual named H. M. Hazelwood on December 25, 1852. Hazelwood was born on February 17, 1848. The inscriptions to Hazelwood are found on both the fonts and the saucer-like plinths. In original condition. Overall height: 7.5". $4,000-$5,000 for the pair.

Palmer Patent spring loaded candle lamp, c. 1850. This device burned a candle having a wick composed of woven wire and cotton that delivered a brighter light than traditional candles. The unusual bell shaped cut and etched blown glass globe is decorated with flowers and leaves. The blown composite glass bulbous standard is white cut to blue. The standard is raised on a gilt lacquered bronze triangular pedestal resting atop scrolled feet. In original condition. Overall height: 28". $2,200-$3,000.

One of a pair of gilt lacquered brass, lacquered brass, and patinated bronze three light Argand chandeliers, manufacturer unknown, second quarter nineteenth century. The coronas are decorated with embossed beading and a crown of palmettes. The three suspension chains that extend from the corona are connected to the base by serpentine figures around reticulated brackets. The burners support rare cut and etched blown glass globes with floral decoration and rolled rims. These globes are thought to be Sandwich glass. The intricately decorated base has applied female masks at the periphery of each burner. The base terminates into a large budding finial. In original condition. Overall height: 31.25". $40,000-$50,000 for the pair.

Detail of the base seen on the previous chandelier.

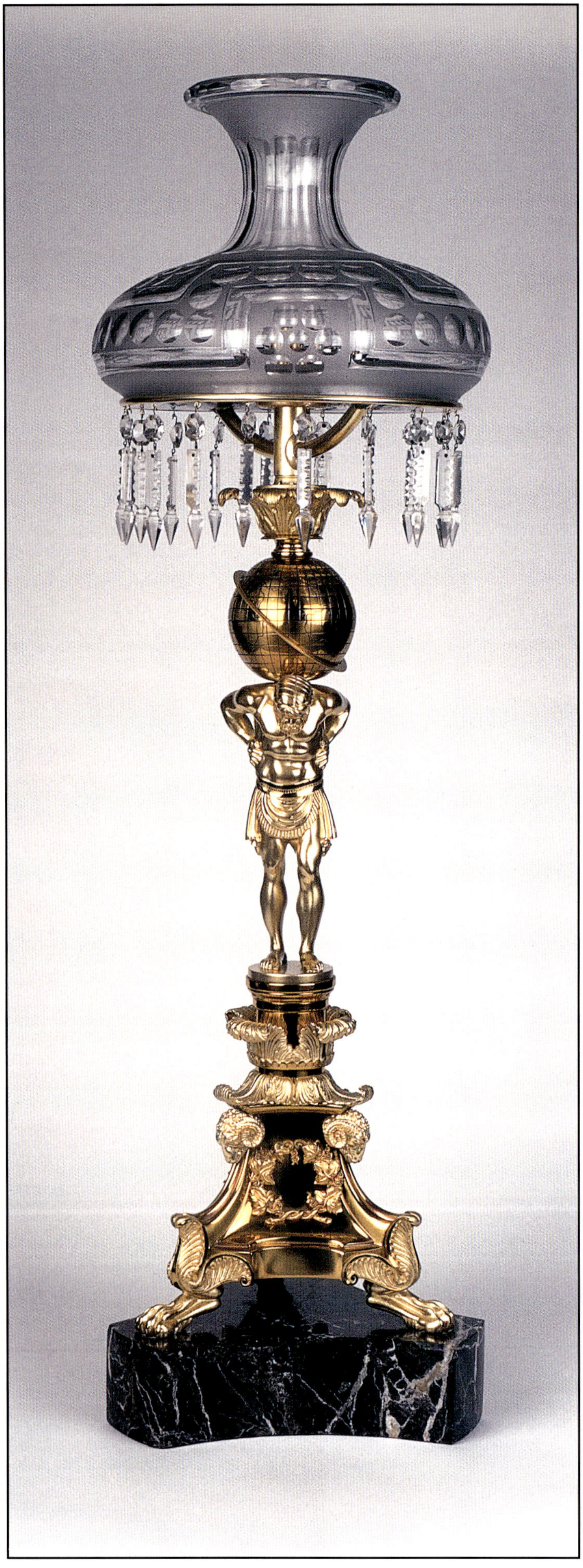

Gilt lacquered brass and bronze and lacquered brass sinumbra lamp, manufacturer unknown, second quarter nineteenth century. The cut and etched blown glass shade is decorated in the Greek key pattern, has a 10" diameter fitter, and faceted neck and rim. Atlas supporting the heavens on his shoulders comprises the standard (see pages 130, 136, 139, and 153 for similar standards). Applied to the base are lions' paws, rams' heads, scrolled leaves, and wreaths. The base and standard are raised on a large octagonal marble plinth. Back-cut Albert pendants are a later addition. The surface is restored. Height to the shade ring: 31" Overall height: 40". $25,000-$30,000.

Detail of glass shade seen in the lamp at right.

Pair of pewter whale oil burning lamps, manufacturer unknown, with an inscription reading: "Rust Patented 1837." The cut and etched blown glass shades are decorated with eagles, American shields, and the Latin motto *E Pluribus Unum* in a banner. In original condition. Overall height: 14". $12,000-$18,000 for the pair.

A plate from an English lighting fixture pattern book demonstrating how different metal castings could be interchanged for candelabras and lamps, c. 1810. This concept has been repeatedly illustrated throughout this book. Left inscription reads: "Candelabra for the dining room." Middle inscription reads: "Candelabra for the gallery." *Courtesy: Victoria and Albert Museum.*

Gilt lacquered brass and patinated bronze sinumbra lamp, manufacturer unknown, probably English or American, second quarter nineteenth century. The font supports a cut and etched blown glass shade that is decorated with alternating berries, leaves, and geometric designs. The shade neck and rim are faceted and the fitter diameter is 10". Scrolled leaves on reeded branches encircle the drip cup. Four separate columns comprise the standard with applied gothic spires mounted between the individual columns. The finely cast base depicts a nun emerging from a cloister door on each of the lamp's four sides. Fleur-de-lis decorate the apex of each door. The standard and base are raised on a triple tiered quatrefoil plinth. In original condition. Height to the shade ring: 25". Overall height: 35.5". $15,000-$20,000.

Opposite page: Detail of plinth and gothic spires seen in the previous lamp.

Detail of nun seen in the previous lamp.

Magnificent dual light patinated bronze Argand lamp, second quarter nineteenth century. The manufacturer is unknown but is possibly the English firm of Messenger and Sons. Messenger patterned many of its works from the Piranesi etchings. One of his illustrations depicts storks very similar to that seen in this lamp. A "No 2" is stamped into the cast iron base weight. Cut and etched blown glass gasolier style shades sit on the shade rings. The scroll handled, urn shaped font is surmounted by a budding floral finial. Branches of anthemia and volutes form the fuel feeder arms. The foliated burner tubes terminate in vasiform drip cups. Acanthus and palmette leaves accent the tapered, reeded standard where three addorsed storks stand at rigorous attention. The acanthi trimmed apophyge rests atop the circular foliated embossed plinth. In original condition. Overall height: 40". $20,000-$25,000.

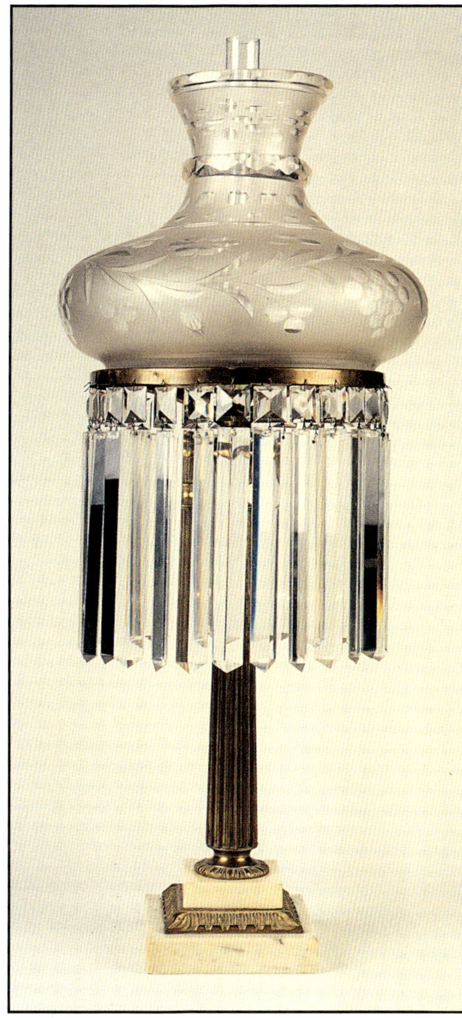

Brass kerosene lamp from the Colonial Revival Period, late nineteenth century, referred to by some lighting authorities as the Second Period. Manufacturer unknown. These lamps are replicas of First Period sinumbras. Colonial pendants hanging from the shade ring are a frequent finding from this era but not earlier (see Overview). The square, double stepped marble plinth supports the reeded brass standard topped with a Corinthian capital. Solar and kerosene lamps made by many different manufactures employ this style plinth but the initial sinumbras did not. The globe is decorated with leaf and berry designs and is from the proper period. In original condition. Height to the shade ring: 20.25". Overall height: 30.25". $3,000-$4,500.

Detail of the kerosene burner and fuel feeder tubes seen in the previous lamp. Note that there are three fuel feeder tubes. Other examples have been found with four fuel feeder tubes. First Period sinumbra lamps had only *two* fuel feeder tubes. Also note the brass font indicating a kerosene burning reproduction (see Overview).

Gilt lacquered brass and bronze and cut crystal sinumbra lamp, American or English, second quarter nineteenth century. The cut and etched blown glass shade has a faceted rim and neck and a 10" diameter fitter. The shade is decorated with geometric motifs. The glass standard contains a silvered brass sleeve and is ornamented with acanthi, terminating on an octagonal stepped plinth. The surface is restored. Overall height: 33". $10,000-$12,000.

Pair of patinated bronze single light Argand lamps, manufacturer unknown, second quarter nineteenth century. Retail label on the burner tubes read: "Lewis Veron & Co. Philadelphia." The cut and etched blown glass shades are decorated with flowers, vines, and berries. Swans with their wings extended are perched atop the prism rings. Georgian pendants are suspended from the fonts. Anthemia and mythological dolphins embellish the bases and triangular plinths. In original condition. Overall height: 15.5". $9,000-$10,000 for the pair.

Top right: Unique gilt lacquered brass and bronze colza burning lamp attributed to W. Blakeway & Son, Birmingham, England, c. 1821. The blown glass shade is raised above the burner by three brackets and is held in place by a set screw. The handle is in the form of a coiled snake. The font rests on three paw feet. The surface has been restored. Overall height: 8.75". $2,500-$3,000.

Bottom right: Dated 1821 W. Blakeway & Son advertisement illustrating various lighting devices including the previous lamp (middle center).

Gilt lacquered brass and patinated bronze solar lamp, manufacturer unknown, c. 1850. The 6" shade ring supports an elegant cut and etched blown glass globe with gothic window designs, rolled rim, and faceted neck. Colonial pendants with snowflake motifs are suspended from the shade ring. The hexagonal standard terminates at the triangular plinth with concave sides. Gilt scrolls are applied to the base of the standard. The plinth is raised on three paw feet. The surface is restored. Height to the shade ring: 18.5". Overall height: 31". $2,500-$3,500.

Gilt lacquered brass and lacquered brass four light gasolier, manufacturer unknown but probably American, second quarter nineteenth century. The central rod descends from the corona and pierces a composite cranberry cut to clear glass vase that is designed in the "Thousand Eye" pattern. Delicate floral chains connect the acanthi decorated corona to the serpentine hooks on the base of the chandelier. The fuel feeder tubes converge into a cranberry cut to clear central dish. The central dish terminates with a large floral finial. The strawberry fan-cut shades are probably a later addition. Otherwise in original condition. Overall height: 36". $20,000-$25,000.

Patinated bronze button lamp, factory converted for camphene use, manufacturer unknown, c. 1840. Three paw feet support the acanthi decorated font that is fitted with a 3-prong camphene burner. A rolled rim, cut etched and blown glass shade decorated with leaves and flowers sits stop the font. An identical lamp is seen in the adjacent catalogue advertisement (right center). In original condition. Height: 21". $700-$800.

Gilt lacquered brass and bronze solar lamp illustrated in the 1850 Hooper catalogue as item No. 493. The 9/16" burner is stamped: "W. F. Shaw 270 Washington Street St Boston." This lamp may well be a product of the Hooper Company or W. F. Shaw. It has been long suspected that Shaw did not have a foundry and obtained his metal castings from larger manufacturers such as the Hooper Company. Alternatively, Shaw advertised solar burner alterations for many different kinds of lamps. The cut and etched blown glass "Oregon" style shade has a 5" diameter fitter and is raised on a foliated standard resting on a square marble plinth. The surface is restored. Height to the shade ring: 11.50". Overall height: 21.5". $1,000-$1,500.

Pair of patinated bronze Argand lamps, manufacturer unknown, second quarter nineteenth century. Acorn finials sit atop the original "tidy caps." The urn shaped fonts have open handles. Square double stepped plinths support the fonts. In original condition. Overall height: 9.5". $6,500-$7,000 for the pair.

Opposite page: To the left is a cut etched molded and blown glass whale oil lamp, attributed to Bakewell and Company, Pittsburgh, c. 1835. The shade and font are decorated in the "Strawberry and Fan" pattern. Overall height: 16". In original condition. $4,500-$5,500. To the right is a rare New England Glass Company sinumbra lamp, second quarter nineteenth century. The cut and etched blown glass shade has a 5.375" wide fitter that rests on a circular font. The standard is gilt lacquered bronze. The pedestal and plinth are molded blown glass. In original condition. Height to the shade ring: 14.75". Overall height: 23.75". $8,000-$12,000.

Detail of burner label that reads: "N. E. Glass Co Boston" seen in the lamp at right.

Pair of gilt lacquered brass and patinated bronze single light Argand lamps, second quarter nineteenth century. Labels affixed to the burner tubes are inscribed with the name of the retailer: "Clark Coit & Cargill N. York." Gilt bud finials with leaves and berries rise from the urn shaped fonts. Spear-tipped Colonial pendants are suspended from the reticulated font rings that are adorned by two hooded personages. The standards are composed of palm leaves growing from octagonal bases topped with volutes. The scrolled plinths are accented with gilt leaves. Gilt tendrils course across the curved, reeded fuel feeder arms toward the delicately cut glass bobeches from which additional spear tipped pendants hang. The cut and etched blown glass shades are decorated with berries and leaves. In original condition. Overall height: 21". $8,000-$10,000 for the pair.

Detail of hooded personages seen in previous lamp.

Detail of burner label seen in previous lamp.

Beautiful French gilt lacquered brass and marble sinumbra lamp, manufacturer unknown, second quarter nineteenth century. A kneeling angel with raised arms comprises the standard. Balanced atop her head is a vasiform drip cup. The embossed 10" shade ring supports a delicate etched glass globe with floral design and an ormolu crown of palmettes. The double stepped marble base is decorated with applied gilt hippocampi and reticulated palmettes. The surface is restored. Overall height: 27.5". $12,000-$15,000.

Pair of gilt lacquered brass and patinated bronze spring-loaded candle lamps, manufacturer unknown, c. 1840. These lamps have never been used ("New Old Stock"). In original condition. Overall height: 21". $1,200-$1,500 for the pair.

Gilt lacquered brass and bronze dual light Argand chandelier, manufacturer unknown, second quarter nineteenth century. The central urn shaped font is decorated with arabesque festoons and a crown of palmettes. The boat shaped dish is highly ornamented with applied leaves, berries, flowers, and masks of Bacchus, the Roman god of wine. A spray of acanthi and berries comprises the bottom finial. The burners support cut and etched blown glass shades with rolled rims. The chandelier is supported by four chains composed of alternating links of varying size that extend between the corona and the dish. The surface is restored. Overall length: 31.5". $15,000-$20,000.

Detail of the bottom seen in the previous chandelier.

Patinated brass and bronze and gilt lacquered brass sinumbra lamp, second quarter nineteenth century. The burner tube bears a label inscribed: "J & I Cox Makers New York E Pluribus Unum." The cut and etched blown glass shade displays lyres. The 10" diameter shade fitter rests on a circular font bordered by a decorative repoussé gilt brass gallery. The columnar standard is raised on a foliated bulbous pedestal, poised atop a square plinth. The lamp is "rumored" to have been in the White House during the administration of William Henry Harrison. In original condition. Overall height: 33.5". $15,000-$20,000.

Detail of the burner label seen in the lamp at right. It is centered by a spread-wing eagle with an American shield upon its breast.

Signed gimbaled lacquered brass colza burning Argand lamp manufactured by Miller and Sons, second quarter nineteenth century. From 1863-1870, their London address was 171 Piccadilly. The surface is restored. Overall height: 16". $1,500-$1,700.

Gilt lacquered brass, French hanging sinumbra lamp, manufacturer unknown, first quarter nineteenth century. Volutes attach to the foliated embossed shade ring forming the suspension brackets. Chains composed of alternating circular and rectangular links connect the volutes to the corona that is decorated with acanthi and palmette leaves. The cut and etched blown glass shade has an 8" fitter diameter and is decorated with small stellate motifs. In original condition. Overall height: 14". $7,500-$8,000.

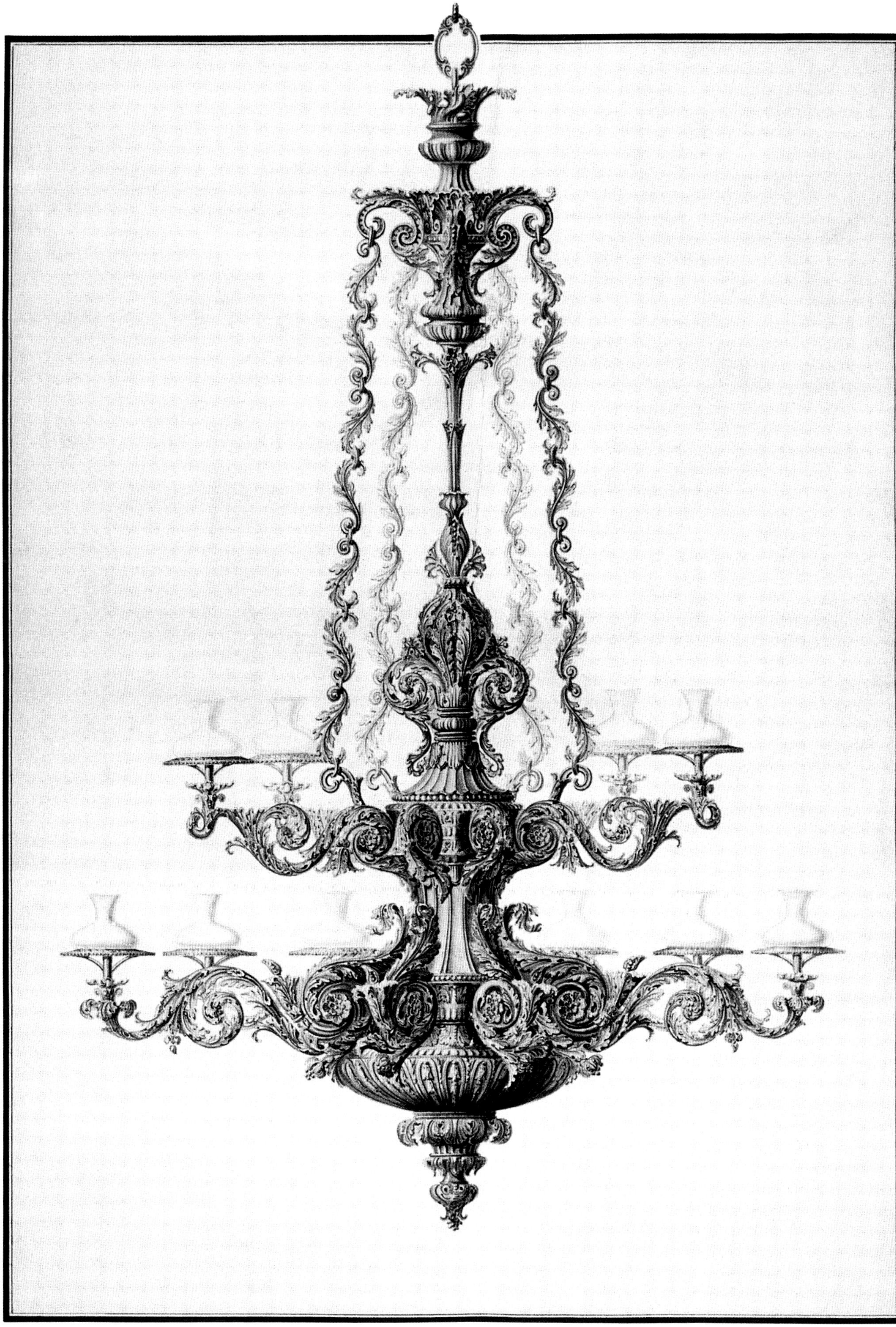

A pattern for an ornate multiple light sinumbra chandelier by Perry and Company, c. 1830. William and George Perry were in the business of producing lamps and lusters until the 1850s. Their address was 72 Bond Street, London England. *Courtesy of the Victoria and Albert Museum.*

Signed pair of English gilt lacquered brass sinumbra lamps, second quarter nineteenth century. The cast iron base weights are stamped: "Birmingham I Ratcliff." John Ratcliff is listed in Wrightson's Directory of Birmingham, England in 1818 as a brass founder on Cannon Street. Each lamp has a foliate decorated baluster shaft on a base in the likeness of Ammon's horn. Cut and etched blown glass shades decorated in the floral and diamond pattern have 10" diameter fitters. The drip cups are trimmed with polished cabochons. The surfaces are partly restored. Height to the shade ring: 23". Overall height: 33.5". $10,000-$15,000 for the pair.

American cut and etched, molded and blown glass oil lamp and matching shade by E. G. Horn, Patent No. 2413, January 8, 1842. In original condition. Overall height: 18". $2,500-$3,500.

This lighting fixture most likely originated as a tin hanging sinumbra lamp with an Argand burner, manufacturer unknown, second quarter nineteenth century. The glassware is a later addition. A similar but clearly not identical lamp is illustrated in the 1850 Henry N. Hooper and Company catalogue as item No. 630. At some point, the Argand burner was converted to one operating on the solar principle (central draft with a deflector—see Overview). The wick is raised by a rack and pinion mechanism. Since the type of burner determines the terminology for the lamp, the correct name for this device now is a hanging solar lamp. Such burner conversions were probably common, as Dietz, Brother and Company of New York and W. F. Shaw of Boston advertised them as early as 1845. The solar burner in this lamp is attributed to W. F. Shaw or William Carleton. Part of Shaw's advertisement in the 1845 Stimpson's Boston Directory reads: "Lamps and Chandeliers of all kinds, altered to Solars with Shaw's improved Patent Shadowless Solar Burner at $1,50 (sic) each…Best solar heads fitted to old astral pedestals for $2." Length from the corona to the drip cup is 26". $3,500-$4,500.

Detail of converted burner found in the previous hanging lamp.

Gilt lacquered brass hanging solar lamp, manufacturer unknown, c. 1850. The cut and etched blown glass shade is decorated with berries and leaves and has an unusually large 7" diameter fitter. The font retains its original burner. Three chains of pierced anthemia connect the foliated brackets to the acanthi decorated corona with a floral finial. Lighting fixtures with very similar suspension chains have been documented in the 1850 Hooper catalogue (see pages 64 and 65). In original condition. Overall height: 42". $3,500-$4,500.

Details of various features seen in the previous chandelier.

Gilt lacquered brass, gilt lacquered bronze, and patinated bronze five light gasolier, manufacturer unknown but probably English, second quarter nineteenth century. This chandelier retains its original pull down chains and counter weights. The reeded central shaft descends downward from the corona into the highly ornamented amalgamation of lions' masks, concave-reeded urns, palmettes, and spread wing eagles that are perched on the edges of the floral encapsulated fuel feeder arms. Delicate chains links connect the eagles' beaks to the foliated branches. Cut and etched blown glass shades in the lyre pattern rest atop the burners. In original condition. Overall height: 38". $30,000-$35,000.

Unusual English gilt lacquered bronze button lamp having a bill of sale dated 1821. These lamps burned both colza and kerosene. The shade is held in place by three coiled snakes. The lamp is modeled after an athenienne, is raised on terms with Bacchus masks, and rests on a triangular plinth. In original condition. Overall height: 16". $2,000-$3,000.

Gilt lacquered brass dual arm spring-loaded candle lamp, manufacturer unknown but probably English, c. 1850. Argand style shades are utilized and a set screw holds them in place. Height to the top of the shade: 25". In original condition. $3,500-$4,000.

Gilt lacquered brass, lacquered brass, and patinated bronze six light gasolier, manufacturer unknown, probably American, second quarter nineteenth century. The corona is in the form of cascading berries. The highly decorated central shaft demonstrates applications of volutes and putti. Emanating from the very elaborate central dish are six sinuous foliated branches, each supporting cut and etched blown glass globes with lyre and leaf designs. In original condition. Overall height: 48". $30,000-$35,000.

Detail of the base seen in the previous chandelier.

On the left is a gilt lacquered brass and bronze solar lamp, manufacturer unknown, c. 1850. The dolphin standard is an unusual feature as is the turban form cut and etched blown glass shade having a 5" diameter fitter. On the right is an argent spelter lamp, illustrated in the c. 1920 Pairpoint catalogue. Both lamps exhibit nearly identical dolphin standards and double marble plinths many years after the initial casting. Both lamps are in original condition. Overall height of both lamps: 19.50". The solar lamp is valued at $2,500-$3,000 and the Pairpoint reproduction at $500-$700.

Gilt brass and lacquered brass four light solar chandelier, manufacturer unknown, c. 1850. Extending from the central baluster are convoluted and highly ornamented branches each supporting a foliated font. Suspended between the grape clustered corona and each branch are four delicate chains composed of connecting clusters of anthemia. Trefoils cap a plain central dish from which a foliated finial projects. The "Oregon" style shades are from a slightly later period. The surface is restored. Overall height: 47". $15,000-$20,000.

Unusually small gilt lacquered brass and bronze solar lamp, manufacturer unknown, c. 1850. The ball shaped cut and etched blown glass top mount shade rests on a 9/16" burner and has a 2.5" wide fitter. The columnar standard is raised on a spreading socle. Height to the top of the font: 7". Overall height: 14". $500-$900.

Gilt lacquered brass, lacquered brass, and patinated bronze solar lamp, manufacturer unknown, c. 1850. The font contains a 3/4" burner. The cut and etched blown glass shade is decorated with oak leaves and acorns. The shade has a faceted neck, rolled rim, and rests on a 6" diameter ring. Albert pendants are suspended from the shade ring. The floral pattern stenciled shaft is topped by an ormolu Corinthian order and is supported on a single marble base. In original condition. Height to the shade ring: 16". Overall height: 29". $2,500-$3,500.

Glossary

Acanthus (-thi): plant from the Mediterranean region having large spiny leaves.
Ammon's Horn: arranged in a spiral similar to a ram's horn; after a ram-headed god of the Egyptians.
Anthemia: ornaments of floral forms in a flat radiating cluster.
Apophyge: small, hollow outward spread at the bottom of a column's shaft by which it joins the base.
Arabesque: ornamentation consisting of combinations of flowers, foliage, fruits, animals, vases, and figures.
Argent: silvery-white color.
Athenienne: a classical brazier set on three monopodia feet with ram's head finials.
Baluster: pillar-like supports.
Breather: a vent in an otherwise airtight enclosure that allows for entry of air.
Cabochon: convex hemispherical form which has been polished smooth but not cut into facets.
Calices: cup or chalice form.
Cartouche: oval tablet with ornamental scrollwork.
Caryatid: female likeness used as a supporting figure.
Central dish: bottom end of central baluster shaft in a chandelier.
Chiton: basic full-length garment worn by women of ancient Greece.
Convolvuli: any of a genus of erect, twining, trailing shrubs of the morning glory family.
Corona: the upper part or crown, particularly the top of chandelier.
Couchant: reclining position.
Diaper design: an allover pattern consisting of repeating units or designs.
Entablature: that part of the architectural order which rests horizontally upon the column.
Festoon: decorative ribbon-like chains or strips hanging between two points.
Fuseau: spindle shaped.
Font: receptacle for fuel; also called a fuel reservoir.
Gadrooned: decorative series of convex and concave flutings and moldings.
Gasolier: gaslight chandelier.

Gimbaled: contrived to keep a suspended object horizontal.

Griffin: mythological animal having the head, forepart, and wings of an eagle and the body, hind legs, and tail of a lion.

Hippocampi: from the Greek mythology meaning sea horse with two forefeet and a body ending in the tail of a fish.

Modillion: ornamental bracket.

Ormolu: gilded metal.

Plinth: block serving as a base.

Putto (-ti): figure of an infant boy.

Quatrefoil: ornamental decorative feature having four lobes.

Repoussé: shaped with patterns in relief.

Reticulated: divided or constructed as to form a network.

Revolute: rolled downward or backward.

Rhyton: a figure shaped in the part like an animal or animal's head.

Rococo: decorative style of the eighteenth century characterized by fancy, curved, elaborate asymmetrical forms.

Roundel: decorative plate, tablet or panel that is round in form.

Smoke bell: small portion of glass which is suspended over the chimney to avert the smoke rising from the burner.

Socle: low plain member supporting a wall or pedestal.

Spelter: zinc.

Standard: structure built to serve as a support; also referred to as stand as in solar stand lamp.

Stellate: star shaped.

Tendril: leaves or stems modified into slender, spiraling, coiled formations.

Trefoil: ornamental decorative feature having three lobes.

Term: pillar that is adorned on the top with a figure of a head or the upper part of the body.

Toupie feet: resembling a spinning top.

Vasiform: shaped like a vase.

Volutes: spiral, scrolled or twisted form.

Bibliography

Bacot, H. Parrott. *Nineteenth Century Lighting: Candle-powdered Devices: 1783-1883.* West Chester, Pennsylvania: Schiffer Publishing Ltd., 1987.

Bourne, Jonathan, and Vanessa Brett. *Lighting in the Domestic Interior: Renaissance to Art Nouveau.* London, England: Philip Wilson Ltd. For Sotheby's Publications, 1991.

Chinnici, R. Curt. *Argand Lighting in Philadelphia, 1800-1845: An Examination of the Manufacturing and Usage of Argand Lamps.* Master's Degree thesis submitted to the Savannah College of Art and Design. Savannah, Georgia, 2000.

Cooke, Lawrence S. *Lighting in America: From Colonial Rushlights to Victorian Chandeliers.* New York City, New York: University Books, 1975.

Cornelius & Baker, Manufacturers of Lamps, Chandeliers & Gas Fixtures, Philadelphia, Reprint by The Rushlight Club, 1999.

Curran, Jean A. *Founders of Carleton College: William Carleton and Susan Willis.* 1916.

Dudar, Helen. "The Grandeur That Was Rome." *Smithsonian,* Volume 31, No.1, April 2000.

Early Lighting: A Pictorial Guide, The Rushlight Club, USA, 1988.

Fennimore, Donald L. *Metalwork in Early America: Copper and Its Alloys.* Winterthur, Delaware: Winterthur Publications, 1996.

Ficacci, Luigi. *Giovanni Battista Piranesi: The Complete Etchings.* New York, New York: Taschen, 2000.

Freeman, Dr. Larry. *New Light on Old Lamps.* Watkins Glen, New York: Century House Publishers, 1968.

Gill, C. *History of Birmingham,* Vol. I (T:B 620), p. 294.

Graham, Frank. *Wrightson's New Triennial Directory of Birmingham 1818.* Norwich, England: Fletcher and Son Ltd., 1969.

Hopkins, E. *Birmingham,* (T:B 620), pp. 46-7, 152.

Leeds City Art Gallery. *Country House Lighting: 1660-1890.* Leeds, England: Leeds City Art Galleries, 1992.

Lamps & Other Lighting Devices, 1850-1906. Des Moines, Iowa: Wallace-Homestead Book Company, 1972.

Maril, Nadja. *Antique Lamp Buyer's Guide: Identifying Late 19th and Early 20th Century American Lighting,* Atglen, Pennsylvania: Schiffer Publishing Ltd., 1998.

Pinn, W. A. and Sons. *Light and Shade: An Exhibition of Antique Lighting and Accessories,* Buckingham, England: Moreton Press, 1993.

The Rushlight, Vol. XII, No. 1: March, 1946; Vol. XLII, No. 1: March, 1976; Vol. XLVII, No. 1: March, 1981; Vol. XLVII, No. 2: June, 1981; Vol. XLVIII, No. 4: December, 1982; Vol. XLIX, No. 1: March, 1983; Vol. XLIX, No. 2: June, 1983; Vol. XLIX, No. 3: September, 1983; Vol. XLIX, No. 4: December, 1983; Vol. 50, No. 1: March, 1984; Vol. 50, No. 4: December, 1984; Vol. 51, No. 4: December, 1985; Vol. 60, No. 2: June, 1994; Vol. 61, No. 3: September, 1995; Vol. 66, No. 2: June, 2000.

Russell, Loris. *A Heritage of Light: Lamps and Lighting in the Early Canadian Home.* Toronto, Canada: University of Toronto Press, 1968.

St. Charles Gallery, Inc. Auction Catalogue. New Orleans, Louisiana, June 1-3, 2001.

Souvenir of Charlestown and Bunker Hill Monument, Boston, 1876.

Thwing, Leroy. *Flickering Flames: a History of Domestic Lighting through the Ages.* Rutland, Vermont: Charles E. Tuttle Company, 1958.

Thuro, Catherine M. V. *Oil Lamps: The Kerosene Era in North America.* Radnor, Pennsylvania: Wallace-Homestead Book Co., 1976.

Thuro, Catherine M. V. *Oil Lamps II: Glass Kerosene Lamps,* Toronto, Ontario: Thorncliff House Inc., 1983.

Watkins, C. Malcolm. *Artificial Lighting In America: 1830-1860.* Washington, D.C.: Smithsonian Institution, 1951.

Wolfe, John J. *Brandy, Balloons & Lamps: Ami Argand, 1750-1803,* Carbondale, Illinois: Southern Illinois University Press, 1999.

Index